SUPERSTARS!™
Heartthrobs

SUPERSTARS!™
Heartthrobs

PRODUCED BY

DOWNTOWN BOOKWORKS INC.

PRESIDENT Julie Merberg
SENIOR VICE PRESIDENT Patty Brown
EDITORIAL ASSISTANT Sara DiSalvo
SPECIAL THANKS Caroline Bronston, Abigail Burden, Esmee Greenfeld, Lola Greenfeld, Sarah Parvis, Arielle Silvan, Simone Silvan, Emily Simon, Paul Thureen, Ava Villalba, Maia Villalba, Hana Woolley, and Emily Zimmerman.

WRITER Sunny Blue
EDITORIAL CONSULTANT Anne Raso
DESIGN Brian Michael Thomas/Our Hero Productions

Time HOME ENTERTAINMENT

PUBLISHER Richard Fraiman
VICE PRESIDENT, BUSINESS DEVELOPMENT & STRATEGY Steven Sandonato
EXECUTIVE DIRECTOR MARKETING SERVICES Carol Pittard
EXECUTIVE DIRECTOR, RETAIL & SPECIAL SALES Tom Mifsud
EXECUTIVE PUBLISHING DIRECTOR Joy Butts
EDITORIAL DIRECTOR Stephen Koepp
EDITORIAL OPERATIONS DIRECTOR Michael Q. Bullerdick
DIRECTOR, BOOKAZINE DEVELOPMENT & MARKETING Laura Adam
FINANCE DIRECTOR Glenn Buonocore
ASSOCIATE PUBLISHING DIRECTOR Megan Pearlman
ASSISTANT GENERAL COUNSEL Helen Wan
ASSISTANT DIRECTOR, SPECIAL SALES Ilene Schreider
DESIGN & PREPRESS MANAGER Anne-Michelle Gallero
BRAND MANAGER, PRODUCT MARKETING Nina Fleishman
ASSOCIATE PREPRESS MANAGER Alex Voznesenskiy
ASSOCIATE PRODUCTION MANAGER Kimberly Marshall

SPECIAL THANKS Christine Austin, Jeremy Biloon, Elizabeth Bland, Stephanie Braga, Jim Childs, Susan Chodakiewicz, Rose Cirrincione, Lauren Hall Clark, Jacqueline Fitzgerald, Christine Font, Jenna Goldberg, Hillary Hirsch, Suzanne Janso, David Kahn, Mona Li, Amy Mangus, Robert Marasco, Robin Micheli, Amy Migliaccio, Nina Mistry, Dave Rozzelle, Adriana Tierno, Vanessa Wu

ISBN 10: 1-60320-937-9
ISBN 13: 978-1-60320-937-3

We welcome your comments and suggestions about Time Home Entertainment Books. Please write to us at: Time Home Entertainment Books, Attention: Book Editors, P.O. Box 11016, Des Moines, IA 50336-1016

If you would like to order any of our hardcover Collector's Edition books, please call us at 1-800-327-6388, Monday through Friday, 7 a.m. to 8 p.m., or Saturday, 7 a.m. to 6 p.m., Central Time.

1 QGS 12

contents

who do you love?

Who's the No. 1 Superstar guy in your heart? Justin Bieber, Taylor Lautner, Diggy Simmons, or anyone of the 5 Brit Boys of One Direction—Harry, Niall, Louis, Liam or Zayn?

Maybe your sigh-guy is someone else, but we bet he's one of the heartthrobs who grace the following pages. Inside you'll find a trivia bonanza with hundreds of facts and tidbits about your favorites, heartfelt quotes from them about crushin' on that special someone, and mega numbers of up-close-and-personal photos! You'll see your faves blinged out in red-carpet finery, chillin' with their friends, running around out and about, and just being themselves. There are even brain-teaser quizzes to test your heartthrob IQ—take 'em yourself or test your BFFs. All together, *Heartthrobs* is a collector's item of fun, fun, fun. So enjoy, enjoy, enjoy!

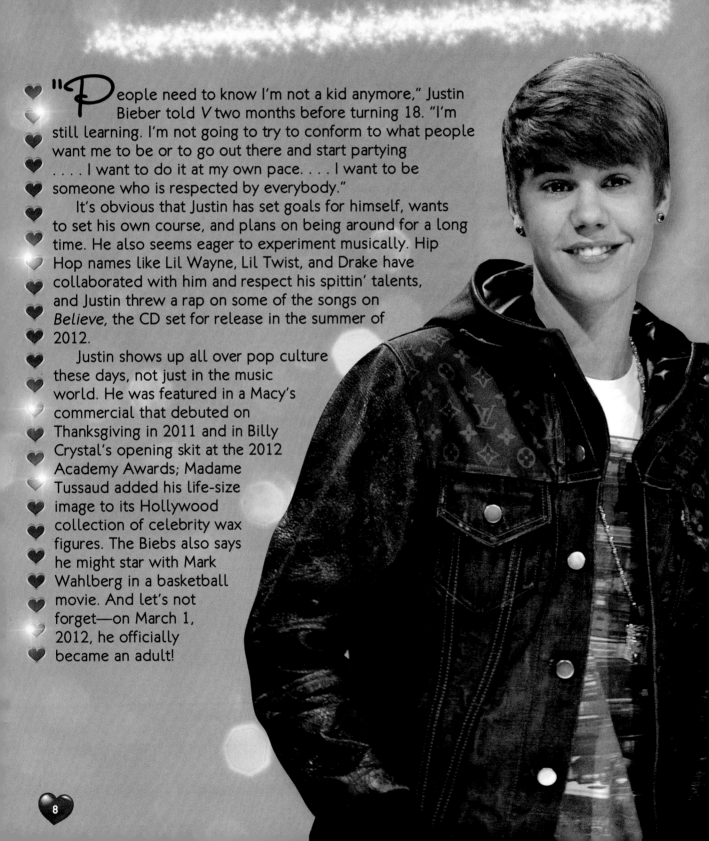

BIEBER-licious

"People need to know I'm not a kid anymore," Justin Bieber told *V* two months before turning 18. "I'm still learning. I'm not going to try to conform to what people want me to be or to go out there and start partying . . . . I want to do it at my own pace. . . . I want to be someone who is respected by everybody."

It's obvious that Justin has set goals for himself, wants to set his own course, and plans on being around for a long time. He also seems eager to experiment musically. Hip Hop names like Lil Wayne, Lil Twist, and Drake have collaborated with him and respect his spittin' talents, and Justin threw a rap on some of the songs on *Believe*, the CD set for release in the summer of 2012.

Justin shows up all over pop culture these days, not just in the music world. He was featured in a Macy's commercial that debuted on Thanksgiving in 2011 and in Billy Crystal's opening skit at the 2012 Academy Awards; Madame Tussaud added his life-size image to its Hollywood collection of celebrity wax figures. The Biebs also says he might star with Mark Wahlberg in a basketball movie. And let's not forget—on March 1, 2012, he officially became an adult!

Justin

justin's girl talk

Want to know what Justin thinks about his boyfriend skills? A lot! "I'm loving and patient and kind and gentle," he told Radio Disney's *Celebrity Take With Jake* in an interview to promote "Boyfriend," his first single from *Believe*. "You just have to be honest with one another. . . that's the first thing, because if you're not honest, then the relationship is just not a good relationship."

That's probably good advice not just for romance, but for relationships with family and friends too.

THE PERFECT DATE: "It's about doing the essential things," Justin told *Twist* "You don't have to spend a lot of money on a date all the time. One thing I love doing is, if you're just chilling, or watching a movie, be like, 'Yo, get dressed, come with me, let's go for a walk.' Then take her for a walk. Girls like when you do spontaneous things."

FIRST DATE: "Don't go to the movies on a first date," he told *Bop*. "You can't talk and get to know each other."

FLIRT ALERT!

"I'm pretty flirtatious, but I don't use any lines," Justin told *Bop*. "I just get my BIEBER on!"

JUSTIN + SELENA = JELENA: Though Justin doesn't have a history of giving in-depth interviews on matters of the heart, he seemed to open up a bit with *New!* in 2011 talking about Selena Gomez. "I wouldn't be with somebody if I wasn't in love," he said. "We were both raised by our moms in single-parent households, and that's given us a lot of the same family values in life."

JB PUNK'D TAYLOR SWIFT

On the premiere of the reworked MTV hit show, *Punk'd,* Justin let everyone see his famous prankster side. The only one who wasn't in on the joke was his good buddy Taylor Swift! In the trailer for the series debut, Justin appears, saying, "I think we should start with Taylor." On the show, the fun began when Justin got Taylor to shoot some fireworks off the balcony of a house on the beach. But the *Punk'd* gang made it look like the fireworks hit a boat in the water. Suddenly there were loud exploding sounds and a wedding party began frantically fleeing the boat. Taylor was horrified, thinking she had not only set fire to someone's property but had ruined a couple's wedding day too! Of course, Taylor had a big heart and forgave her pal JB when she found out it was all set up!

Taylor Swift

the best of bieber

Justin recently signed new artist Carly Rae Jepsen to his label School Boy. He first noticed her music when he was hanging out with Selena Gomez, the guys from Big Time Rush, and Ashley Tisdale. Joking around, they lip-dubbed a video to the song "Call Me Maybe" by one Carly Rae Jepsen. And then, Justin told Ryan Seacrest on his LA radio program, "I looked [Carly Rae] up and I [saw] she wasn't signed and so I signed her. Right now, I am focusing on one [artist] at a time . . . that's what Usher did with me and he helped me tremendously."

This is a real brain-teaser—you HAVE to be a true Justin fan because the info is NOT in the previous pages!

Justin got another tattoo last winter—an image of Jesus on the calf of his left leg. His other tattoos include a seagull on his hip that was inspired by the book *Jonathan Livingston Seagull*. Justin told yahoomusic.com, "It's a book my family all reads. My dad has it. My grandma has it. My cousins have it." Justin also has the name of Jesus written in Hebrew on his right side—his dad has the same one.

Justin's 18th birthday party at L.A.'s Regent Beverly Wilshire Hotel was a celeb-o-rama with Kim Kardashian, Kylie and Kendall Jenner, boxer Mike Tyson, Ashley Tisdale, Cody Simpson, and many more incredible stars on the guest list!

What's your J.B. I.Q.?

Fill in the blanks, if you can!

1. The name of Justin's fragrance collection is _____.

2. Justin's best school subjects are _____ and _____.

3. Everyone knows Justin likes soccer, hockey, and basketball, but some would be surprised he also likes to get out on the links and play _____.

4. Justin's favorite color is _____.

5. Justin loves the fruit-flavored _____ breath mints.

6. As a boy back in Canada, Justin says, he grew up listening to Michael Jackson and the group _____.

7. Justin's favorite comedian/actor is _____.

8. Justin tweeted about his all-time favorite birthday present (pre his Fisker Karma car). It was a _____.

9. Justin played a bad boy on this TV drama series: _____.

10. Scooter Braun, Justin's manager, discoverd JB on what popular website?: _____

Answers: 1. Someday; 2. English and math; 3. golf; 4. purple; 5. Certs; 6. Boyz II Men; 7. Will Ferrell; 8. purple pool table; 9. CSI; 10. YouTube

OUT & ABOUT

Whether it's a night of Hollywood glamor or a shopping stroll in New York City's Soho district, celebrity couples hold hands, snuggle, laugh, and travel thousands of miles to be with each other! Check out some of your faves just being themselves.

tom felton + jade olivia

Harry Potter star Tom Felton and his longtime girlfriend, Jade Olivia, recently made the move from England to California. They met on the set of *Harry Potter and the Half-Blood Prince*, where she was the stunt coordinator's assistant. Her role changed when the *Harry Potter and the Deathly Hallows—Part 2* producers thought the couple would create sparks onscreen and cast Jade as Astoria Greengrass, Draco's wife in the final film's epilogue.

austin butler + vanessa hudgens

Long-distance romance? Working on *Spring Breakers* in Florida didn't deter Vanessa Hudgens from seeing BF Austin Butler while he shot *The Carrie Diaries* in New York City. They kept the airways busy jetting back and forth north-to-south and south-to-north during their hectic schedules!

andrew garfield + emma stone

Andrew Garfield and Emma Stone first met in 2010 when they were filming *The Amazing Spider-Man*. At the time, Andrew had plenty of wonderful things to say about his costar. "I really do like Emma, she's a pretty special actress and a pretty special person," he told *Extra*. "[She's] one of the funnier people and one of the more fun-loving people I know." Then in the summer of 2011, the two were spotted doing what couples do: holding hands in Central Park and out enjoying dinner for two. And they still seemed to be going strong in 2012 at the Nick Kids' Choice Awards. Amazing!

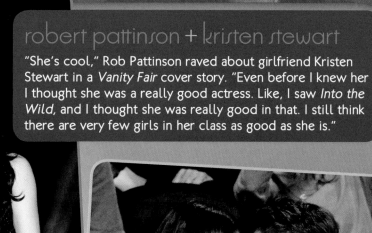

robert pattinson + kristen stewart

"She's cool," Rob Pattinson raved about girlfriend Kristen Stewart in a *Vanity Fair* cover story. "Even before I knew her I thought she was a really good actress. Like, I saw *Into the Wild*, and I thought she was really good in that. I still think there are very few girls in her class as good as she is."

justin bieber + selena gomez

"Everybody can see [Selena] is hot and that's great, but there is so much more to her than that," Justin told *New!*. "She makes me laugh and she puts up with my practical jokes."

liam hemsworth + miley cyrus

During an *On Air With Ryan Seacrest* interview, *Hunger Games* star Liam Hemsworth said his girlfriend, Miley Cyrus, was cheering on his success. "[Miley] is one of the biggest stars in the world—there's no shadowing her," he said. "She embraces [my new fame]. She's very, very happy for me."

inside BIG TIME RUSH

Ever since James Maslow, Logan Henderson, Carlos Pena, Jr., and Kendall Schmidt first appeared on Nickelodeon as Big Time Rush in January, 2010, they have been on the go! Their schedule has consisted of 12-hour film days, five days a week, and no time off on the weekends. Saturday and Sunday have been devoted to studio time, recording music for the series and their albums. With their third season of *Big Time Rush* under way in 2012, the band had already released two albums, *B.T.R.* and *Elevate*, and filmed five TV movies—*Big Time Audition, Big Time Concert, Big Time Christmas, Big Time Beach Party,* and *Big Time Movie*. On the last movie, a riff on the Beatles' movies, they gained permission to sing four Beatles songs. And in February 2012, they started their Better With U Tour in Las Vegas before heading out to crisscross the United States. "We can't wait to hit the road again!" the guys said in a press release. These guys like to keep moving!

JAMES ON CAMARADERIE IN THE BAND: "We're really good friends, which is really a blessing. I hear horror stories of other shows and groups who don't get along and all of us are like brothers. Off set, we'll get together for dinner and talk about the show, but since we spend about 16 to 18 hours a day together, we try to talk about other things!" *(Bop)*

Big Time Rush

btr: heart-2-heart secrets

Right now James, Logan, Carlos, and Kendall say they are too busy to settle down, but you'd still like to know what the boys think about matters of the heart—wouldn't you? Hear it straight from them. . . .

KENDALL: "If you're convinced [a certain girl] is the one for you . . . try a gesture to wow her. I sent one girl a lot of flowers. . . . I'm a romantic person. It's pretty amazing to find a dream girl. I try to grab her hand, pinkie-to-pinkie, and then if she doesn't question it, ring finger to ring finger. You have to take it slow." *(Bop)*

CARLOS: "I think there are different levels of love. I was only really in love with one girl when I was younger. But, I've also loved others in a different sense. . . . I've loved girls because they've always been there for me as friends. But I think you'll know when you really fall in love because something inside will tell you." *(Twist)*

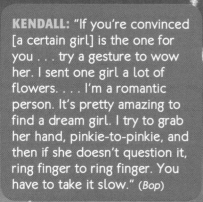

JAMES: "The first real kiss I had was on a school trip with my English class in sixth grade. It was the first time I stayed in a hotel with a bunch of friends. Fifteen of us met up in a room and we were playing Seven Minutes in Heaven and I got picked! We couldn't leave the room! It got awkward kissing in front of everyone! It was more like Seven Seconds of Fear! After that, I was like, 'I feel better about kissing now. I'm moving up in life!'" *(Bop)*

LOGAN: "My freshman year of high school, I got paired up with this senior girl for a play. She was like, 'We should do a scene with a kiss in it. It'd be so cute!' I had a huge crush on her. We were practicing the skit at her house and I kissed her for the first time. I was so excited but really nervous." *(Bop)*

more heart-2-heart secrets

LOVING LOGAN

"I give out a lot of compliments! I notice things and call attention to what's great about her. I'm not afraid to say what's on my mind!" *(Bop)*

"A girl with an accent is NEVER a bad thing! Whenever they speak, you're like, 'I have no idea what you're saying, but you sound really cute when you say it!'" *(Bop)*

"Be goofy. Make me laugh!" *(Bop)*

JAMES . . . FROM THE HEART

"'Love is a strong word. I've used it with very few people in my life. It's a big deal." *(Twist)*

"I like being friends first before getting into a relationship. Then the awkwardness is gone!" *(Tiger Beat)*

"I've honestly met girls with braces and found them cute because they have braces. I've never had braces, so maybe that's the attraction. *(Bop)*

CUTIE CARLOS

"I like being a romantic. I like to be sweet, open the car door and take a girl to dinner." *(Tiger Beat)*

"I was 13 and at summer camp when I had my first real kiss." *(seventeen)*

"If a girl cooked for me—that'd be awesome! I love a nice homemade lasagna!" *(Bop)*

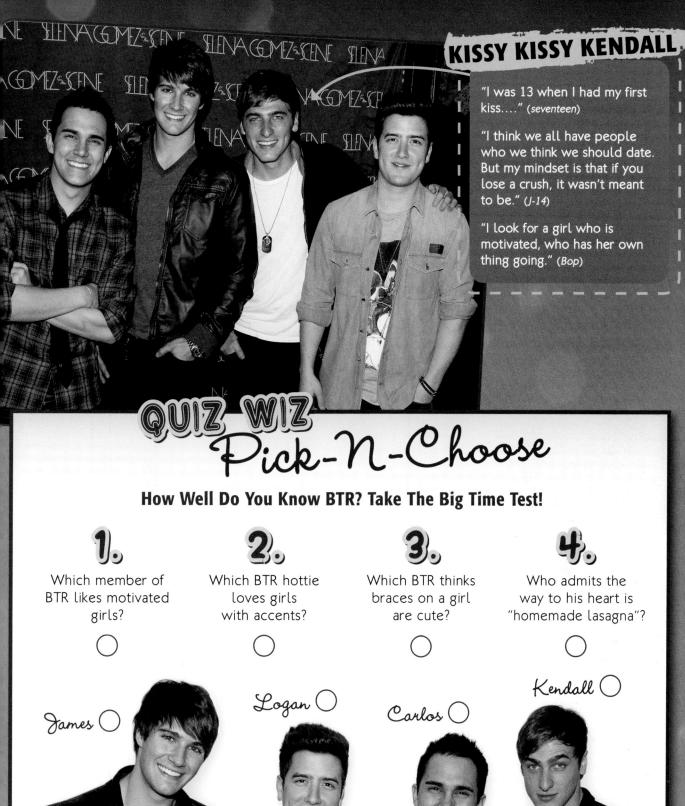

"I was 13 when I had my first kiss...." (*seventeen*)

"I think we all have people who we think we should date. But my mindset is that if you lose a crush, it wasn't meant to be." (*J-14*)

"I look for a girl who is motivated, who has her own thing going." (*Bop*)

QUIZ WIZ
Pick-N-Choose

How Well Do You Know BTR? Take The Big Time Test!

1. Which member of BTR likes motivated girls? ◯

2. Which BTR hottie loves girls with accents? ◯

3. Which BTR thinks braces on a girl are cute? ◯

4. Who admits the way to his heart is "homemade lasagna"? ◯

Kendall ◯

James ◯ Logan ◯ Carlos ◯

Answers: 1. Kendall. 2. Logan. 3. James. 4. Carlos.

rocket to (BRUNO) MARS

His real name is Peter Gene Hernandez and he hails from Honolulu, though his family moved to L.A. after he graduated from high school. Bruno has spent nearly all his life involved with music. He started by doing Elvis impersonations for family gigs at the age of 3! "Everybody in my family sings, everyone plays instruments. My uncle's an incredible guitar player, my dad's an incredible percussionist, my brother's a great drummer; he actually plays in our band. I've just been surrounded by it." Eventually, Bruno began to write and produce songs for other artists, signing on to Motown Records. In 2009, Bruno moved to Elektra/Atlantic Records, released his debut solo album *Doo-Wops,* and blew up. He became a best-selling digital artist in 2011. Fans definitely love him "just the way he is!"

Bruno

the love songs of bruno mars

Bruno is successful at mixing musical styles and making them mainstream. He even bucks current trends by embracing a style that had its heyday more than 50 years ago, doo-wop. His father grew up in Brooklyn, which was a mecca for doo-wop, and turned him on to the golden oldies! Bruno loves the simplicity of those songs.

But love songs are always part of Bruno's repertoire, too—and his female fans are grateful! Many of his lyrics are based on his own personal relationships. He doesn't mind being called a sensitive guy and is an avowed fan of female singer-songwriters like Alicia Keys—as well as the more romantic tracks released by a certain Mr. Justin Bieber.

TOUGH NAME, TENDER HEART

What would it be like if you were Bruno's arm-candy?

Bruno says with a chuckle that being famous gives him confidence with the ladies. He told AOL Music, "Why be famous if you can't go, 'Excuse me, I don't know if you know me, but I am a big deal. I'm the "Grenade" guy!'"

Bruno says he never takes a lady for granted and believes in giving lots of compliments!

He may not look like a typical heartthrob, and his lyrics are certainly less flowery, but Bruno can be just as heart-melting as Romeo with his Juliet.

Bruno's fans love to sing these particularly tender lines from "Just The Way You Are": "Her lips, her lips, I could kiss them all day if she'd let me/Her laugh, her laugh she hates but I think it's so sexy."

Bruno doesn't mind being called a "gushy guy"—but he likes to point out that he can rock as well!

He says that the ultra-sweet "Nothin' On You" is one of the songs he's most proud of because of the "beautiful lines" and he thinks it was a key factor in getting his record deal.

Bruno's big on the lyrics of undying love sung by the classic teen idols and boy bands. He likes Justin Bieber (with whom he's worked), New Edition, NKOTB, and 'N SYNC.

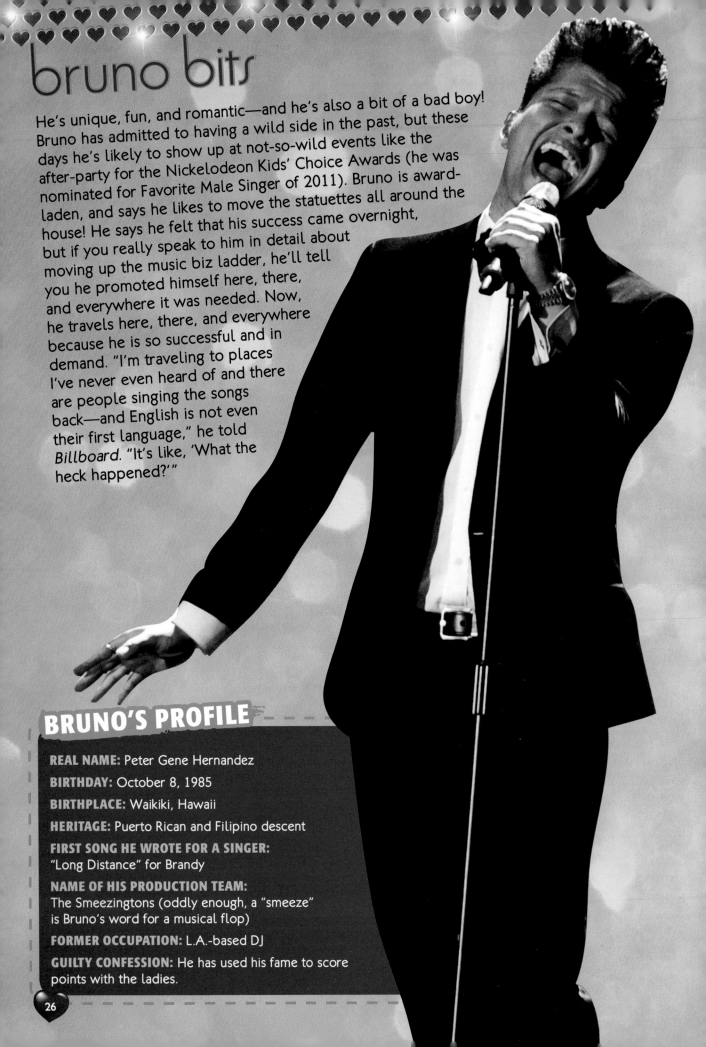

bruno bits

He's unique, fun, and romantic—and he's also a bit of a bad boy! Bruno has admitted to having a wild side in the past, but these days he's likely to show up at not-so-wild events like the after-party for the Nickelodeon Kids' Choice Awards (he was nominated for Favorite Male Singer of 2011). Bruno is award-laden, and says he likes to move the statuettes all around the house! He says he felt that his success came overnight, but if you really speak to him in detail about moving up the music biz ladder, he'll tell you he promoted himself here, there, and everywhere it was needed. Now, he travels here, there, and everywhere because he is so successful and in demand. "I'm traveling to places I've never even heard of and there are people singing the songs back—and English is not even their first language," he told *Billboard*. "It's like, 'What the heck happened?'"

BRUNO'S PROFILE

REAL NAME: Peter Gene Hernandez

BIRTHDAY: October 8, 1985

BIRTHPLACE: Waikiki, Hawaii

HERITAGE: Puerto Rican and Filipino descent

FIRST SONG HE WROTE FOR A SINGER:
"Long Distance" for Brandy

NAME OF HIS PRODUCTION TEAM:
The Smeezingtons (oddly enough, a "smeeze"
is Bruno's word for a musical flop)

FORMER OCCUPATION: L.A.-based DJ

GUILTY CONFESSION: He has used his fame to score points with the ladies.

BRUNO'S BIGGEST GROOMING SECRET: Bruno uses margarine, berries, and potato chips blended together for maximum volume in his hair.

BRUNO ON HIS TATTOOS:
"[One is] my mother's name on my arm, Bernadette. The first one I ever got, I was 19; it was a sacred heart. I got it upside down (though)!"
(rap-up.com)

Bruno's TRUE OR FALSE

Do you think you know Bruno THAT well?
Test yourself with our quick Q&A!

1. Bruno used to work as an Elvis impersonator.
TRUE OR FALSE?

2. Bruno's production team is called the Sneezing Fools.
TRUE OR FALSE?

3. His first professional song was written for Brandy.
TRUE OR FALSE?

4. He's a fan of Alicia Keys.
TRUE OR FALSE?

5. He was once signed to Motown Records.
TRUE OR FALSE?

6. "Just The Way You Are" is a tribute to Billy Joel.
TRUE OR FALSE?

7. He was the top best-selling digital artist worldwide in 2011.
TRUE OR FALSE?

8. His father is originally from Brooklyn.
TRUE OR FALSE?

Answers: 1. True; 2. False; 3. True; 4. True; 5. True; 6. False; 7. False; 8. True.

six degrees of SUPERSTAR love

From Hollywood to Paris, from Sydney to New York, it's a small world for teen celebrities: Boy meets girl, girl meets boy, boy goes out with another boy's girl, on and on, and everyone changes partners! Just think of high-school dating, but played out in the glare of the paparazzi's cameras. You could get whiplash trying to track the love lives of your favorite SUPERSTARS! To help you out, we've provided this handy-dandy Romance-o-gram.

Austin Butler

Zac Efron

Josh Hutcherson

Vanessa Hudgens

josh + vanessa

Did Josh Hutcherson and Vanessa Hudgens indulge in real-life romance in 2011? Or, as some Hollywood gossips insist, was it just part of a plan to promote *Journey 2: The Mysterious Island*, the 2012 film in which they costarred? Josh did nothing to clear up to the confusion when he and Vanessa were interviewed on the Australian *Today* show. Asked if they were a couple, Josh awkwardly answered, "We're not. We were at one point, but she broke my heart. No, I'm just kidding. That was a while ago. We're really good friends now."

Taylor Swift

Taylor Lautner

zac + lily

"I like humor and spontaneity, and something you wouldn't expect," Zac told people.com about relationships. "I'm a big practical joker, and you can make [practical jokes] very romantic." Maybe that's why he and Lily Collins starting hanging out in February 2012. The girl likes a sense of humor! "Prince Charming is someone that can make you laugh no matter what," she said during a press conference for her film, *Mirror, Mirror.*

Lily Collins

taylor + selena

Taylor Lautner and Selena Gomez first met in Vancouver, Canada in 2009 when he was filming *Twilight Saga: New Moon* and she was making *Ramona and Beezus.* Kristen Stewart introduced them when Taylor visited Kristen at her hotel, the same one where Selena was staying!

Selana Gomez

SPOTLIGHT ON
AUSTIN BUTLER

Once known for being an adorable cutie on Nickelodeon and Disney Channel comedies, Austin Butler has fast-forwarded on our screens, cast in the CW network's new series *The Carrie Diaries*—and become a full-fledged heartthrob in the process! The California born-and-bred star of *Aliens in the Attic* knows how to show off his romantic side for the girls, but he's also good at bringing on the giggles and is never afraid to laugh at himself. Austin is a dream boy-next-door!

AUSTIN'S MOST EMBARRASSING ON-SCREEN MOMENT:
Aliens in the Attic: "We were up on the roof filming. It was so embarrassing because it was one of the easiest lines in the entire movie, and for some reason, I kept mixing the words wrong. We did so many takes! I felt so bad. I got it right at the end but I got Ashley [Tisdale] laughing at me, Carter [Jenkins] was laughing at me. My stomach was in a knot."
(BOP)

HEAD-2-TOE FACT FILE

FULL NAME: Austin Robert Butler

BIRTHDAY: August 17, 1991

BIRTHPLACE: Anaheim, California

PARENTS: Lori and David Butler

SIBLING: Older sister, Ashley

FIRST REGULAR ACTING JOB: Zippy Brewster on Nickelodeon's *Ned's Declassified School Survival Guide*

FEATURE FILM: *Aliens in the Attic*

TV SERIES: *Zoey 101, Ruby & The Rockits, Life Unexpected, Switched At Birth, The Carrie Diaries*

TV MOVIES: *Betwixt, Intercept*

INSTRUMENTS: Guitar and piano

PETS: Two Chihuahuas, Delilah and Sofia

FAVORITE BOOKS: *Adventures of Huckleberry Finn* by Mark Twain, *The Giver* by Lois Lowry, *The Time Machine* by H.G. Wells, *Nineteen Eighty-Four* by George Orwell

SECRET TALENT: Can bounce on a pogo stick as long as he wants to!

AUSTIN'S DREAM DATE:
"Sometimes the best dates are spontaneous adventures. I've had a lot of great dates, but one that sticks out in my mind started out as what was supposed to be a tame night going to a house party with this girl. We ended up being bored by the party, so we left and took two guitars and skateboards and skated around the USC campus for a while, which is beautiful at night, then played guitar for two hours on this grassy knoll. After that we weren't tired, so we went to this 24-hour diner by the beach where we ate and decided to go swimming afterward. Then we walked down to the beach, swam in the ocean, and then sat in the sand and talked until the sun came up. It was a nice night."
(Troix)

AVAN JOGIA & LEON THOMAS

Avan Jogia and Leon Thomas III, the heartthrobs of Nickelodeon's *Victorious*, are—according to fans of the show—totally dream-worthy. They sing, dance, act, and best of all, they like to reach out to their fans to get to know them better. They consider the followers of the show BFFs. And speaking of best friends . . . while Leon's character, Andre, is best friends with Victoria Justice's lead character Tori, Avan is the actress' best friend in real life! Read on to discover what you might share with Leon and Avan!

HEAD-2-TOE FACT FILE

FULL NAME: Avan Tudo Jogia

BIRTHDAY: February 9, 1992

BIRTHPLACE: Vancouver, Canada

NICKNAME: Sweet Eyes—*Victorious* costar Victoria Justice gave it to him.

PARENTS: His mom was born in Canada and is of Irish and Welsh descent; his father was born in London and is of Gujarati Indian descent.

SIBLING: Older brother, Ketan

HEIGHT: 5'10"

WEIGHT: 140 lbs

PET: Jack Russell Terrier named Max

BEST FRIENDS: Victoria Justice and Josh Hutcherson

INSTRUMENTS: Guitar and piano

FIRST CONCERT: Backstreet Boys

FAVORITE HISTORICAL FIGURE: Gandhi

FAVORITE HOBBY: Photography

GIRL TALK

look for someone who is caring, empathetic, and understanding . . . and always wants to learn."
(NICK News Video)

Victorious cast members team up with the National Wildlife Federation and the Thomas Starr King School in L.A. for Nickelodeon's The Big Help.

HEAD-2-TOE FACT FILE

FULL NAME: Leon G. Thomas III

BIRTHDAY: August 1, 1993

BIRTHPLACE: Brooklyn, New York

PARENTS: Mother, Jayon Anthony (singer and dancer), and father, the late Leon G. Thomas, Jr. (a jazz singer)

BROADWAY PRODUCTIONS: *The Lion King; Caroline, or Change;* and *The Color Purple*

FILM: *August Rush*

TV SERIES AS A COSTAR: *Victorious*, and *The Backyardigans* (as the singing voice of Tyrone)

INSTRUMENTS: Guitar, piano, drums, bass, sax, and beatbox

MUSICAL EXTRA: Leon has his own channel on YouTube—"Leonthomasmusic"

MUSICAL INFLUENCES: Michael Jackson, Stevie Wonder, Donny Hathaway, Prince

SONG HE WROTE FOR VICTORIOUS SOUNDTRACK: "Song To You"

SURPRISING PASTIME: Karaoke

FUN FACT: Leon performed his original song, "Countdown," on the February 18, 2012 episode of *Victorious*.

FAVORITE HOBBY: Bike riding

FAVORITE MUSICAL ARTISTS: Prince, Kings of Leon

GIRL TALK

"I look for personality—the fact that she can have a cool conversation with me and we can go on for hours laughing . . . the fact that she can take a joke."
(NICK News Video)

SP TLIGHT ON JAKE SHORT

Jake Short costars on the Disney Channel series *A.N.T. Farm* as Fletcher Quimby, a middle-school art prodigy who has a mad crush on Chyna Parks, played by China Anne McClain. While his character isn't much of a smooth operator when it comes to love, off the set, Jake's not short on the qualities that make a guy a real sweetheart. Just take a look!

The words Jake found the most difficult to pronounce when he was little were "spaghetti," which he called "pagetti," and "hamburger" which he called "hambooger."

HEAD-2-TOE FACT FILE

FULL NAME: Jacob Patrick Short

NICKNAME: Jake

BIRTHDAY: May 30, 1997

BIRTHPLACE: Indianapolis, Indiana

PET: Part-Chihuahua rescue mutt, Skipper

INSTRUMENT: Guitar

FAVORITE PASTIMES: Playing basketball, soccer, or martial arts

FAVORITE PRO ATHLETES: Tim Tebow, Peyton Manning

FAVORITE BANDS: Blink-182, Vampire Weekend, Death Cab for Cutie

FAVORITE BOOKS: The Hunger Games trilogy

FAVORITE MOVIE BASED ON A BOOK: *The Hunger Games*

FAVORITE SCHOOL SUBJECT: Chemistry

PERSONAL MOTTO: Never give up

Unlike his TV character, Fletcher, Jake says, "I have no artistic talent at all, so that is our main difference, but I enjoy girls so we have that in common!" *(Pixie)*

When Tyler Blackburn first started playing Caleb on *Pretty Little Liars*, he was listed as recurring, but in early 2012, Tyler got a promotion and became a regular on the series. The Burbank, California, native considered that the best day of his life . . . so far.

Indeed, there's much more to come for Tyler, who told *Huffington Post* that he's considering branching out into music. "I've always been into music. It's kind of like a common thread in my life. . . . It's something I've thought about doing professionally for a while now." In pursuit of that dream, Tyler wrote, sang, and made a video of "Save Me," for the web series, *Wendy*.

TYLER TALKS ABOUT THE PERFECT FIRST DATE:
"I really like relaxed, comfortable, nice dinners . . . or a picnic at the beach, something like that. Somewhere you can talk, laugh and have fun."
(lenalamoray.com)

HEAD-2-TOE FACT FILE

FULL NAME: Tyler Blackburn

BIRTHDAY: October 12, 1986

BIRTHPLACE: Burbank, California

HERITAGE: European and Native American

HEIGHT: 5'10½"

TV SERIES: *Unfabulous, Days of our Lives, Pretty Little Liars*

WEB SERIES: *Wendy*

EARLY CAREER: Model

FAVORITE ACTIVITIES: Hiking, traveling, cooking, yoga

FAVORITE SINGER: Matt Corby

FAVORITE VACATION SPOT: Kauai, Hawaii

FAVORITE ACTORS: Dustin Hoffman, Emile Hirsch, Johnny Depp

FAVORITE RELAXATION: Doing yard work at his home

FAVORITE CHICK FLICK: *The Notebook*

TYLER TALKS ABOUT BULLYING: "I'm now a supporter of Stomp Out Bullying, and I was able to go to … Washington D.C. to raise awareness about cyber-bullying and bullying. . . . Being a little bit more of a public figure, it's sort of awesome when you can lend a hand to certain charities and that type of thing." (WeLoveSoaps.com)

TYLER TALKS ABOUT FLIRTING: "It's funny—I don't really know when a girl is flirting with me. I'll go talk to a girl and have it be friendly, and she's gorgeous, but then I'll leave and my friends will be like, 'Where are you going?!?' and I'll be like, 'Oh, I thought she wasn't interested.' I'm not normal when it comes to that whole thing. It's a big game, and I don't like playing it too much." (seventeen)

TYLER'S *PRETTY LITTLE LIARS'* EXPERIENCE: "It has been dream-like and surreal how great it has been. I have wanted to be an actor for a long time. I feel like this is such a great show. . . . This is like a dream come true. I am so excited to go to work. It's just ideal. I think particularly because I am doing what I love and want to do in life." (Pixie)

SP TLIGHT ON
ROSHON FEGAN

One of Roshon Fegan's nicknames is 3inaRo (pronounced three-in-a-row) because he sings, he acts, and he dances. But calling him a triple-threat entertainer doesn't really cover it, because he also writes songs, raps, and plays five instruments—including the ukulele!

The phenom had some inspiration from his family: his father, Roy, is a longtime actor, writer, and producer. Roshon was 12 when he got his first movie credit, a small part on *Spider-Man 2*. Then he became known for his role as Sander Loyer in the Disney Channel *Camp Rock* movies. Now he's a Disney favorite starring as Ty Blue on *Shake It Up!* And he made time to appear on the 14th season of *Dancing with the Stars*—where his moves proved swoon-worthy!

"I always notice a confident girl. Being confident is key." *(Bop)*

HEAD-2-TOE FACT FILE

FULL NAME: Roshon Bernard Fegan

NICKNAMES: Ro or 3inaRo

BIRTHDAY: October 6, 1991

BIRTHPLACE: Los Angeles, California

PARENTS: Cion and Roy Fegan

HERITAGE: Filipino and African American

PET: Dog named Chase

FUN FACT: Roshon can speak Tagalog, the main language of the Philippine Islands

TALENTS: Acting, dancing, singing, rapping, songwriting

INSTRUMENTS: Drums, piano, guitar, ukulele, keytar

MUSICAL INFLUENCES: Michael Jackson, Bruno Mars, B.o.B.

FANS' NICKNAME: Robots

FAVORITE SAYING: It's Ya Boy, Ro!

"I started playing drums at about 7 or 8. My mom used to let me play with the pots and pans and instead of telling me to stop like most moms would, she just let me do it. So the noise kind of turned into music."
(thecelebritycafe.com)

"I like girls that are funny. If you can make me laugh, let's hang out."
(Bop)

Roshon calls his musical style "Hip-Pop"—a combination of Hip Hop and Pop.

SPOTLIGHT ON SPENCER BOLDMAN

"Spencer Boldman: The Hottest Guy You Haven't Heard Of Yet" read an October 2011 headline on fanquarterly.com. Well, that was then . . . this is now. Already starring as Adam on Disney XD's *Lab Rats*, Spencer made a career leap to the big screen in early 2012 in the hit comedy *21 Jump Street*. If you want to become an expert on Spencer, commit all of this to memory!

SPENCER'S PERFECT DATE

"A girl who knows how to have a good time and doesn't take herself too seriously."
(seventeen)

HEAD-2-TOE FACT FILE

FULL NAME: Spencer Thomas Boldman

BIRTHDAY: July 28, 1992

BIRTHPLACE: Dallas, Texas

CURRENT RESIDENCE: Los Angeles, California

PARENTS: Laura and Mike Boldman

SIBLING: Older brother, Jake

FIRST PET: Dog named Max

HIGH SCHOOL SPORT: Lacrosse

FIRST MOVIE: *Bambi*

FIRST ALBUM BOUGHT: Backstreet Boys

COLLECTIONS: Baseball cards

FAVORITE PRO TEAM: New England Patriots

FAVORITE ACTORS: Paul Newman, Leonardo DiCaprio

FAVORITE ACTRESSES: Carey Mulligan, Jessica Chastain, Kate Winslet

FAVORITE MUSICAL ARTISTS: John Mayer, The Dave Matthews Band, Ellie Goulding, Adele

FAVORITE ICE CREAM: Vanilla

FAVORITE BOOK: *Moby Dick*

ASTRO

Astro had a rocky start on *The X Factor*. After his initial success, he landed in the bottom two of the competition and had to participate in a sing-off with fellow contestant Stacy Francis. At the time, some people called him arrogant and cocky. But he regained his composure, apologized to the audience and judges and eventually earned the seventh-place spot on the debut season of the show. Since then, his trajectory has been high. He signed a record deal with *X Factor* judge L.A. Reid and Epic Records, was a featured artist on Cher Lloyd's "Want U Back" single, and landed a guest role on the TV series *Person Of Interest*. Then, at the age of 15, the rapper started working on his debut album, which he hopes to release in 2012. "I'm very excited, I'm ecstatic; it's beyond exclamation," he told *Vibe*. "It feels like a job and it feels fun. It's just pretty dope!"

HEAD-2-TOE FACT FILE

REAL NAME: Brian Bradley

NICKNAME/STAGE NAME: Astro, which is short for Astronomical Kid

BIRTHDAY: August 26, 1996

BIRTHPLACE: Brownsville, New York

RAP/BUSINESS IDOL: Jay-Z

FANS' NICKNAMES: Team Astro or Astronauts

ORIGINAL SONG HE PERFORMED ON *THE X FACTOR*: "Stop Looking at My Mom"

FAVORITE FILMMAKER: Spike Lee

MYSTERY MOLLY

During one X Factor show, Astro called out to his girlfriend, Molly, but he won't talk about her to reporters!

ON BEING ON *THE X-FACTOR*: "I've learned a lot from it. It got me mad; it got me happy; it got me sad. It was just a great experience. I wouldn't change a thing." (*The X Factor* exit interview)

SP⭐TLIGHT ON THE WANTED

The U.K. boy band, the Wanted, first conquered the charts in England and the rest of Europe and now they're gunning for America. Their first two studio albums, *The Wanted* and *Battleground*, both earned gold album status in the U.K., and the spring 2012 release of *The Wanted* in the U.S. is expected to follow suit.

When Max George, Jay McGuiness, Siva Kaneswaran, Tom Parker, and Nathan Sykes arrived in the U.S. in January 2012 for their first mini-tour, they opened for Justin Bieber and soon found themselves surrounded by fans—including British soccer superstar David Beckham and his singer wife, Victoria Beckham. They even became friends with the tour's headliner. After all, as pop sensations, the Brits and the Biebs have a lot in common. But that doesn't mean they talk shop. "When we speak to him," Max told MTV News, "it's more we talk about football or basketball." Hmm . . . Is that American football or Beckham-style?

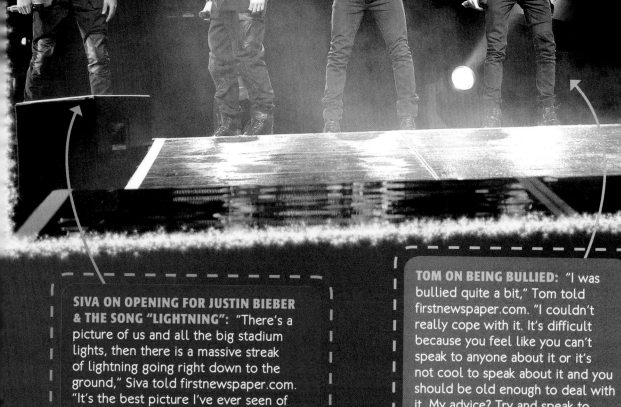

NATHAN ON BEING CALLED "THE BABY" OF THE BAND: "That's cool—the girls love it," Nathan said to *OK!*. "They also call me the quiet one of the band. I'm a bit of an old man really. I just sit in the corner with a nice cup of tea!"

MAX ON BEING A BOY BAND: "We're not bothered what you call us," Max told *OK!*. "We're just average lads, from working-class backgrounds.... We haven't changed the way we live. As long as we don't get called 'man band' just yet—that sounds a bit strange!"

JAY ON SCHOOL: "I was quite a big kid at school," Jay told firstnewspaper.com. "Quite overweight. I really liked English. I wasn't natural at maths so I was a bit scared of it."

SIVA ON OPENING FOR JUSTIN BIEBER & THE SONG "LIGHTNING": "There's a picture of us and all the big stadium lights, then there is a massive streak of lightning going right down to the ground," Siva told firstnewspaper.com. "It's the best picture I've ever seen of us. And that's where the song 'Lightning' came from. Ha ha, it wasn't really!"

TOM ON BEING BULLIED: "I was bullied quite a bit," Tom told firstnewspaper.com. "I couldn't really cope with it. It's difficult because you feel like you can't speak to anyone about it or it's not cool to speak about it and you should be old enough to deal with it. My advice? Try and speak to someone as soon as possible."

SPOTLIGHT ON
LUCAS CRUIKSHANK

Lucas lives in Columbus, Nebraska, with his parents and seven brothers and sisters and started making videos with his mom's camera when he was 12 years old. He and his cousins, Jon and Katie Smet, created spoofs of horror movies and talk shows. At first they were just for fun, for family and friends. Then Lucas and his cousins started posting them on YouTube.

When Lucas was 13, he conjured an annoying, speedy-voiced, 6-year-old character named Fred Figglehorn, based on his two younger brothers. "They were crazy little kids, and I exaggerated what they did and made Fred like them. I get a lot of ideas living in a huge family," he told people.com. Lucas shot videos of himself as Fred and started posting those videos on YouTube—and that's when Lucas suddenly found himself with a following.

"It was so surprising," Lucas told cosmogirl.com. "I wasn't expecting anyone to watch them. I really didn't understand YouTube, so I didn't know that anyone could watch them besides my friends! Then they started getting tons of views and I was so surprised. I guess kids were passing it to their friends on MySpace and Facebook and everything. It just kind of blew up—I was really lucky."

Talent and persistence may have had something to do with it too. Lucas, who always wanted to be an actor, turned Fred into an industry! He appeared as himself and Fred on *Hannah Montana* and on *iCarly*, starred in two series, *Fred* and *Figgle Chat*, and two TV movies, *Fred: The Movie* and *Fred 2: Night of the Living Fred*, and continued the saga on Nickelodeon with the 2012 series *Fred: The Show*. A third movie is in the works, and after high school graduation in May 2012, Lucas was planning on moving out to L.A. to pursue his career in acting, writing and producing.

HEAD-2-TOE FACT FILE

FULL NAME: Lucas Alan Cruikshank

BIRTHDAY: August 29, 1993

BIRTHPLACE: Columbus, Nebraska

PARENTS: Molly and David Cruikshank

SIBLINGS: Five older sisters and two younger brothers

PETS: Four dogs, two cats, two cockatiels

HOUSEHOLD DUTIES: Mows the lawn and feeds the animals

FIRST CAR: Chrysler Seabreeze, handed down to him from one of his older sisters

FIRST BOOK HE READ: *Green Eggs and Ham* by Dr. Seuss

FAVORITE HOME COOKED MEAL: Mac & Cheese

FAVORITE BOOKS FOR TEENS: *Kite Runner, Diary of a Wimpy Kid, Harry Potter* series

FAVORITE BANDS: Linkin Park, 3OH!3, Cobra Starship

the epic
TAYLOR LAUTNER

Taylor Lautner has come a long way since 2005, when he was in *Cheaper by the Dozen 2* and *The Adventures of Sharkboy and Lavagirl in 3-D!* Back then, he was a cute, karate-loving kid. In The Twilight Saga series, we have seen Taylor grow from a sweet teen into a certified Hollywood hottie! The *Breaking Dawn* movies show Taylor and Jacob mature. "I was really excited about [*Breaking Dawn: Part 1*], because Jacob becomes a man," Taylor told *Pixie* magazine.

Taylor is often asked about his exercise and health regime . . . and asked to show his "guns." But whether you are on Team Jacob or a Taylor Tot you know there's a lot more to Taylor than his looks. He's smart too—he tested out of high school in 2008, one year early, and started taking online college courses. Taylor is definitely the full heartthrob package!

TAYLOR'S FIRST KISS

"It was sometime in junior high . . . I think it was just a random girl from school. I mean, it's not like I walked up to her and was like, 'You're just a random girl and I'm going to kiss you,' but just a girl from school, and we had a little thing in junior high."
(seventeen)

Taylor

taylor lautner's super swag

Promoting *Breaking Dawn: Part 1* at 2011's Comic-Con, Taylor told fans, "I'm super jealous of my CGI wolf. It's pretty cute and fluffy."

Well . . . a lot of girls think Taylor is pretty cute too! Though fluffy—not so much! Of course, it takes a lot more than being cute to be a major heartthrob like Taylor. It's also about that certain indescribable something in a guy's walk, his talk, his personality, the way he looks at a girl, especially a girl who's lucky enough to have his attention! Whatever it is, Taylor's got it!

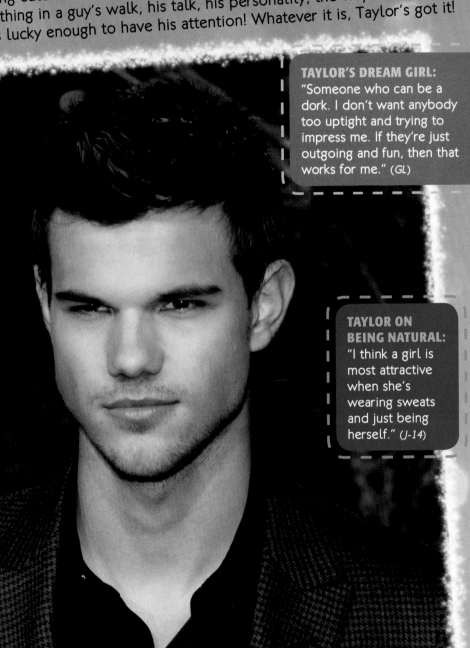

TAYLOR'S DREAM GIRL:
"Someone who can be a dork. I don't want anybody too uptight and trying to impress me. If they're just outgoing and fun, then that works for me." (*GL*)

TAYLOR ON BEING NATURAL:
"I think a girl is most attractive when she's wearing sweats and just being herself." (*J-14*)

Lily Collins

Kristen Stewart

SHHH! TAYLOR'S PALS TELL ALL!

"He's literally like a puppy," Kristen Stewart told *GQ Australia* about Taylor. "There [was] a lot of downtime on [the *Twilight*] set. I'd throw food in his mouth. Taylor is like one of those wind-up toys. You put 20 cents in and he runs around, then he crashes. At lunch, he has a Red Bull and he's back up. When I hear him talk about girls it's like, Awww."

"He's a talented actor and a gentleman," Lily Collins told *seventeen* magazine. "Taylor is very humble. He has so many fans and he never forgets that. He really appreciates the support that he's gotten through the years, and he gives it right back. To me, that makes a good leading man."

TAYLOR ON TALKING TO A GIRL:
"I guess it just depends on the girl. Sometimes I'll feel free to completely open up, and I wish I could do that more often because that's what I look for in a girl. Someone [who] can open up and be herself." (*seventeen*)

TAYLOR ON BEING ROMANTIC:
"I always bring a girl roses before a date." (*QuizFest*)

LOL with taylor

Taylor trivia ahead, plus a quiz that will tell you if you're the type of girl Taylor dreams of!

TAYLOR ON SINGING: "I'm a big fan of all those singing competition shows. Most recently, I've been into *The Voice*. It's one of my secrets!. . . Personally, I sing for fun, but mainly in the shower, when I'm alone. Other people definitely do not want to hear me sing." *(seventeen)*

TAYLOR ON INTERNET GOSSIP: "It's very rare that things [you read on the Internet] are true about yourself.... It's just sad sometimes. So you definitely try and stay away from it as much as possible." *(Parade)*

Taylor's first audition as a kid was for a Burger King commercial—he didn't get the part.

EYE ON TAYLOR

FULL NAME: Taylor Daniel Lautner

BIRTHDAY: February 11, 1992

BIRTHPLACE: Grand Rapids, Michigan

CURRENT RESIDENCE: Valencia, California

PARENTS: Deborah and Daniel Lautner

SIBLING: Younger sister, Makena

HERITAGE: German, French, Dutch, and Native American (Ottawa and Potawatomi tribes)

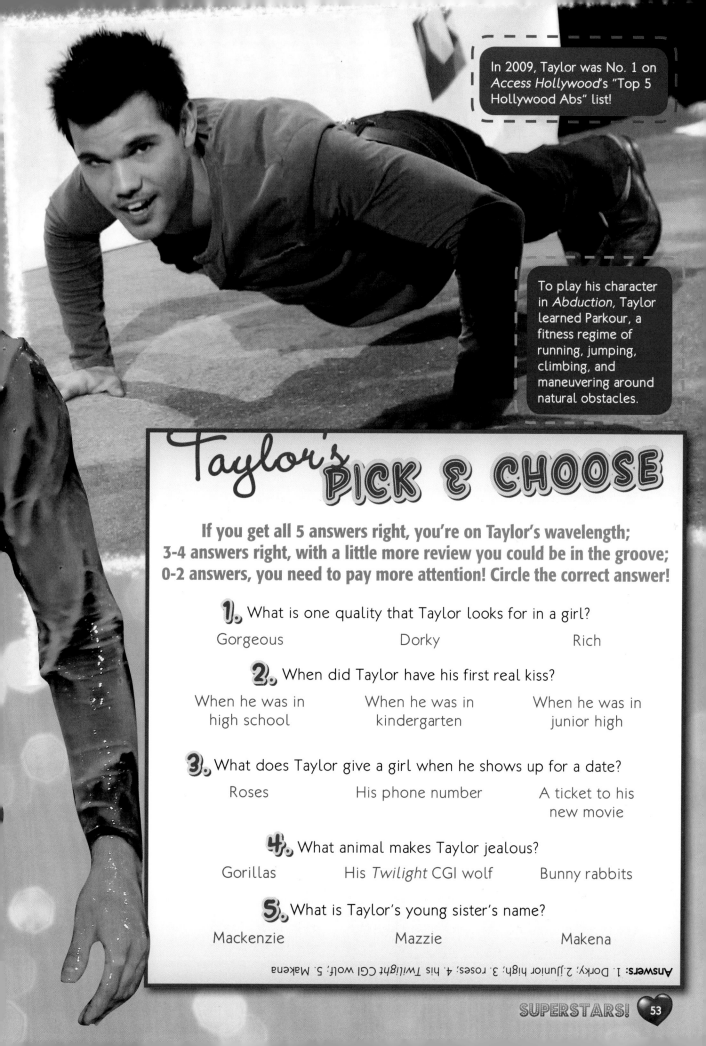

In 2009, Taylor was No. 1 on *Access Hollywood*'s "Top 5 Hollywood Abs" list!

To play his character in *Abduction*, Taylor learned Parkour, a fitness regime of running, jumping, climbing, and maneuvering around natural obstacles.

Taylor's PICK & CHOOSE

If you get all 5 answers right, you're on Taylor's wavelength; 3-4 answers right, with a little more review you could be in the groove; 0-2 answers, you need to pay more attention! Circle the correct answer!

1. What is one quality that Taylor looks for in a girl?

Gorgeous   Dorky   Rich

2. When did Taylor have his first real kiss?

When he was in high school   When he was in kindergarten   When he was in junior high

3. What does Taylor give a girl when he shows up for a date?

Roses   His phone number   A ticket to his new movie

4. What animal makes Taylor jealous?

Gorillas   His *Twilight* CGI wolf   Bunny rabbits

5. What is Taylor's young sister's name?

Mackenzie   Mazzie   Makena

Answers: 1. Dorky; 2.junior high; 3. roses; 4. his *Twilight* CGI wolf; 5. Makena

KARATE HOTTIES

Three of these four hot actors have big-time karate backgrounds that got them the hook-up for martial arts-themed TV hits and one is a quick learner! There are the three fabulous *Kickin' It* teens: luscious Leo Howard, who's been a champion in martial arts since the age of 4; adorable Alex Jones, who got tips from his sister, Alexis, who has an advanced green belt in Tae Kwon Do; and delectable Dylan Riley Snyder, who picked up the basics of karate in a two-week boot camp before the series started. Then there's Ryan Potter, a sexy Nick TV *Supah Ninja* and Japanese-American prize-winning martial artist. Ryan is a walking encyclopedia of Japanese culture—he lived in Japan until the age of 6 and is sad that his Japanese is getting a little rusty!

leo howard

KICKIN' IT WITH A BLACK BELT

FULL NAME: Leo R. Howard

NICKNAME: Hazard

BIRTHDATE: July 13, 1997

BIRTHPLACE: Newport Beach, California

HEIGHT: 5'4"

NOT-SO-SECRET SECRET: He does all his own stunts on TV and also excels in gymnastics

HOMETOWN: Fallbrook, California

AGE AT WHICH HE FIRST STARTED MARTIAL ARTS: 4

BLACK BELT STATUS: He's won three world championships, and has a black belt in his specialty, Shorin-ryu

PARENTS: Randye and Todd Howard

WORD HE MISPRONOUNCED AS A LITTLE KID: Banana (he'd just say "nana")

CHARITY WORK: Volunteers at a vet clinic

MOTTO HE LIVES BY: Follow your dreams!

BIG HOLLYWOOD BREAK: *Kickin' It*

alex jones

ON ACTING COOL WHEN MEETING *KICKIN' IT!* COSTARS LEO HOWARD AND JASON EARLES (TWO DISNEY LEGENDS): "When I went into the studio, I just acted like they were my coworkers instead of being a big fan. They were great!"

HE'S GOT ALL THE RIGHT MOVES

Alex gets his kicks in many ways, not just through karate. However, he is determined to become accomplished in martial arts. "When we were in the middle of [*Kickin' It's*] season one and season two hiatus, I took Tae Kwon Do and actually got my advanced white belt," He told yahoo.com. "I was pretty excited about that."

dylan riley snyder

FIVE FACTOIDS ON A "HEAVY HITTER"

Dylan's Milton in *Kickin' It* is his first comedic role. Believing diverse skills are important for actors, Dylan hopes to try singing at some point.

His favorite karate kicks are the tornado kick and the spinning back kick. The latter is the famous Bruce Lee move that combines spinning around and kicking with your leg. You have to be in fierce shape to do it!

Dylan explained to *Starry Constellation* that he got involved with *Kickin' It* because "I always just wanted to get a kick into the TV aspect of acting and this job came at me from left field and I just had to say yes."

The most challenging thing about being on *Kickin' It* for Dylan is that he has to keep his character nerdy *and* cool! He says it's tough finding the middle ground between being confident and feeling like an outsider.

The Alabama native plans on going to college. Most of his family are alumnae of the University of Alabama so that's a possibility, but he hopes to apply to other schools as well, including NYU, Harvard, and Yale.

ryan potter

THE ABC'S OF RYAN POTTER

R is for refrigerator, where Ryan keeps his juice and leftovers (not to mention his favorite prepared foods from Trader Joe's).

Y is for "Y not"—his general attitude about trying new things!

A is for is for actors that he loves, including Robert Downey, Jr., Jeff Bridges, and Zooey Deschanel!

N is for ninjas! He's one of the hottest TV ninjas of all time!

P is for Poifull, his favorite candy from Japan, where he first grew up.

O is for "Oh so hard!" That's his description of math class!

T is for tech toy—his favorite is his iPhone.

T is also for Toddland, the hipper, younger line by his favorite designer, Todd Oldham, that he can't get enough of.

E is for Eric Carle, one of his favorite authors, best known for *The Very Hungry Caterpillar*.

R is for @RyanKPotter, his Twitter handle—tweet him and tell him that SUPERSTARS sent ya!

playing games with
JOSH HUTCHERSON

Ask anyone who knows Josh Hutcherson . . . he's funny! He loves joking around with his friends and having a good time. But for Josh, it's not all fun and games. He's pretty determined, too. While he was still in elementary school, he decided he wanted to act. "[My parents] were always the ones saying, 'You can be whatever you want when you grow up, the world is yours; and, as your parents, our job is to make that possible: to make your dreams come true,'" Josh told *Nylon Guys*. "So when I told them I wanted to be an actor, they were like, 'Umm, OK. We don't really know how to go about this, but let's try it.'"

It's safe to say he more than tried it. First he starred in TV movies such as *Miracle Dogs* and *Eddie's Father*. Then he landed parts in films like *The Polar Express, Little Manhattan, Zathura: A Space Adventure, Bridge To Terabithia, Journey To The Center Of The Earth, Cirque du Freak: The Vampire's Assistant, The Kids Are All Right, Journey 2: The Mysterious Island, The Hunger Games*, and the upcoming *Red Dawn*.

For Josh, this is just the beginning. "I want to get into directing and producing and writing my own stuff at some point," he told MTV News. "It's all about balance; everything in life is about balance."

Josh

the boy next door

Wouldn't it be nice to have a next-door neighbor just like Josh? He's cute, he's talented, and, most of all, he seems really down-to-earth. If you like a guy who's not afraid to express his feelings, who loves simple dates like walking on the beach at night or dinner and a movie, well, Josh is your kind of guy!

IS HE SIMILAR TO PEETA WHEN IT COMES TO GIRLS?: "Peeta has a hard time saying how he feels to women. I have the opposite problem. I say it too soon, so we're different in that respect. . . . I think I should probably adopt more of Peeta's strategy and maybe play it cool a little longer." (MTV News) Although . . .

"I'm horrible at talking to girls for the first time, so there is that element that I can relate to as far as me taking that first initiative to talk to a girl. I've never really had that dying love for someone and not told her. Not yet at least." (*Justine*)

WHAT KIND OF GIRL DOES HE GO FOR?: "I like feisty girls who can really hang with guys. . . . She's got to be willing to hop on the back of the steel horse [his motorcycle]! Sorry, that's a must!" (*InStyle*)

WHAT'S THE KEY TO WINNING HIS HEART?: "For me, it's all about being true to yourself and being real. I think if a girl tries to be something she's not, to try and make you think otherwise of her, then that's just unattractive. I'd much rather be with somebody that's naturally who they are." (celebuzz.com)

HOW EASILY DOES HE FALL IN LOVE?: "Like that [snaps fingers]! I'd rather have loved and lost than not loved at all. So when I'm in a relationship, I'm very 'I love you, I love you, I love you!'" (*InStyle*)

Josh with *Hunger Games* costar, Jennifer Lawrence, at the L.A. premiere.

JENNIFER . . . SWEET ON JOSH: "Josh is the kind of guy who would do anything for anybody. He's loyal, sweet, and hilarious. His style is very individual, but charming and cool." (*InStyle*)

"Josh. . . . Josh is Peeta. He's charming, he's nice, he's very real and down-to-earth. He's not fake in any way. He just can charm anyone and anything." (*MTV News*)

JOSH . . . SWEET ON JENNIFER: "[Jennifer] is literally 180 degrees different from Katniss," Josh told MTV News. "It's amazing, honestly, to watch her effortlessly flip back and forth, because she's very fun, very hilarious. And to watch her on 'Action!' go boom, right into the character is kind of impressive . . . . She's talking and being Jennifer up until they're rolling sound and when they say 'Action!' boom, [she goes] right into character."

JOSH + VANESSA: While making *Journey 2: The Mysterious Island* together, Josh and Vanessa Hudgens reportedly dated. Josh told *seventeen*, "When I first met her, we just really hit it off. We could be goofy and silly and not worry about anything except having fun."

hungry for hutcherson facts?

Dig in! Then test yourself and see how you do.

In *The Hunger Games*, Josh's character is a baker's son. In real life, Josh knows his way around the kitchen. "I can [bake], actually. I do a really good French apple pie—the whole shebang, including the crust. And I made a couple of loaves of bread when I was visiting Kentucky, where I'm from. . . . I just wanted to make bread. . . . But I'm really more of a grill guy—I do great burgers." (*InStyle*)

Josh had to put on 15 pounds of muscle for the role of Peeta. He worked out with a Navy SEALs trainer five days a week for one month, pulled car tires filled with weights across the gym room, and pounded a punching bag with a baseball bat until he nearly dropped!

Josh's first attempt at entertaining people was when he was 5 years old and sang the Brooks & Dunn song "Boot Scootin' Boogie" at the Boone County Fair back home in Kentucky.

As a toddler, Josh carried a blanket he called Yellow Blankie with him everywhere.

Josh has a Harley-Davidson Forty-Eight motorcycle. He personalized it by having the tank painted midnight blue with an outline of Kentucky on it.

JOSH'S QUICKIE STICKIES

BIRTHDAY: October 12, 1992

BIRTHPLACE: Union, Kentucky (population 5,379)

ASTRO SIGN: Libra

FAVORITE NOVELS: *The Catcher in the Rye* and *To Kill a Mockingbird*

FAVORITE LITERARY CHARACTER: Holden Caufield in *The Catcher in the Rye*

SCRAMBLED Josh

See if you can unscramble the words that are meaningful to Josh!

1. BTAIHITREA
(HINT: Josh once crossed the bridge to this place)

2. EDLOHN FUACELDI
(HINT: Josh's favorite book character)

3. SINSAKT
(HINT: Josh loves playing games with her)

4. LLOEYW IKNALBE
(HINT: Josh carried this everywhere)

5. LERYAH-OSDNIAVD
(HINT: Josh loves to ride this)

Answers: 1. TERABITHIA; 2. HOLDEN CAUFIELD; 3. KATNISS; 4. YELLOW BLANKIE; 5. HARLEY-DAVIDSON

HUNGER GAMES HUNKS

jumpin' jack quaid

As the son of actors Meg Ryan and Dennis Quaid, 20-year-old Jack Quaid is very familiar with the whole movie scene. "I've been on sets my whole life," he told MTV News. But when he took on the role of Marvel, one of the tributes in *The Hunger Games*, his perspective changed dramatically, from someone watching from the sidelines to someone participating in the action. "[For me] this is the first time in front of the camera and not in a chair with Sour Patch Kids from the craft services truck. It was a new sensation. It was weird . . . I really liked it," he said.

Jack's *HG* character is not likely to be a fan favorite. As a matter of fact, he told *Interview*, "I do something horrible to someone very small and cute, and then I have my [butt] handed to me immediately after. . . . When I got cast, I was told that people would be spitting on me in the streets."

Marvel may win no hearts onscreen, but Jack Quaid may soon be collecting them offscreen! Want to get to know him a little bit better? Here's some must-know info!

JACK'S STATS

FULL NAME: Jack Henry Quaid

BIRTHDAY: April 24, 1992

BIRTHPLACE: Los Angeles, California

COLLEGE: The Experimental Theatre Wing of the Tisch School of the Arts at New York University

SIDE JOB: Stand-up comic

SHORT FILM: *Sitting Babies*

LEAST FAVORITE FOOD: Junk food—but he ate loads of hamburgers and milkshakes to bulk up for his *Hunger Games* role

THE BOY CAN MOVE: "He can dance," says *Hunger Games* costar Isabelle Fuhrman about Jack. "I have a really great video of him dancing to 'Single Ladies.'" *(J-14)*

luscious alexander ludwig

In the 2009 movie *Race To Witch Mountain*, Alexander Ludwig played Seth, one-half of the alien brother-sister duo (AnnaSophia Robb played his sister, Sara). Well, Xander has grown up a lot since then! He glowed on the big screen as Cato, the fearsome tribute who battled Katniss in *The Hunger Games*. To get in shape for the role, the Canadian actor told *VMan*, "I needed to get jacked, so I ate like a caveman and lifted heavy weights almost every day. To gain muscle, dieting is just as important as the actual working out, if not more so. I also wanted to keep an eight-pack so I had to bike a lot and do a ridiculous amount of sit-ups." All for our viewing pleasure!

ALL ABOUT ALEXANDER

NICKNAME: Xander

BIRTHDAY: May 7, 1992

BIRTHPLACE: Vancouver, Canada

PARENTS: Sharlene and Harald Ludwig

SIBLINGS: Younger twins, Natalie and Nicholas, and younger sister, Sophie

COLLEGE: University of Southern California— theater major

BEST HG FRIEND: Jack Quaid

SELF-DESCRIPTION: "My heart lies in music and acting," he told *Bello*.

FAVORITE BOOKS: *Harry Potter* series

FIRST CONCERT: Backstreet Boys

PETS: A dog named Waverly and a cat named Puss In Boots

LUCKY NUMBER: Seven—because he was born on May 7, at seven minutes to 7:00, and weighed 7 lbs. 7 oz.

BEHIND-THE-SCENES FUN: "As soon as I found out I got the offer [for *The Hunger Games*], I started hitting the gym," Alexander told *Justine*. "I wanted Cato to have as much of a physical presence as he did a mental one."

team LIAM

Much has changed for Liam Hemsworth since playing the role of Gale in *The Hunger Games*. Instead of being known as "that cute Australian actor" who's been Miley Cyrus's hot BF, Liam is now an object of fascination in his own right! No wonder he says he'd love to do *The Hunger Games* sequels!

Liam's character, Gale, manages to survive in the woods, but could Liam do it in real life? "I grew up wrestling sharks and fighting crocodiles," he told toofab.com. "It's kind of second nature." (We think he was joking!)

The 6'3" Aussie did get rattled by one creature he encountered while filming. He told mtv.com, "We had a black bear on the set and that was a little scary." Considerably less scary is Ziggy, the adorable rescue mutt Miley gave Liam in January 2012 for his birthday!

When Liam first took Miley to Oz (that's a nickname for Australia), she was a little weird about the food. He told justjaredjr.com he got her to try meat pies, "the only thing she liked there. They're like chicken pot pies but only with beef. On top of the meat pieces was macaroni and cheese. They're pretty much the best thing ever."

Liam

liam: hot! hot! hot!

Liam is a full-fledged heartthrob now, but he didn't get off to such a great start with women. If you go all the way back to his school days in the Land Down Under, you'll see he first needed some lessons in wooing the girl of his dreams. In first grade he had a crush on a girl named Amanda, but he didn't know how to express his feelings. Apparently, some of his friends were crushing on Amanda, too, but they didn't have a clue, either. "We'd throw sticks at her across the playground—anything to get her attention!" he told *seventeen*. "I probably treated her more mean than nice, because I didn't know what to do."

He's learned a thing or two since then, judging from his closely watched relationship with Miley Cyrus. Their romance has been tracked in the press from the moment they met in 2009 on the set of *The Last Song*, to their first kiss filming that movie, to their breakup in 2010 and reconciliation in 2011 to. . . . Who knows what the future holds? When a heartthrob gets together with a SUPERSTAR, you know it's going to be exciting, one way or the other!

But don't talk to him about being a heartthrob! "I don't consider myself a heartthrob in any way," he told reporters at *The Hunger Games* premiere. Hmm. . . Come to think of it, Amanda from first grade might agree!

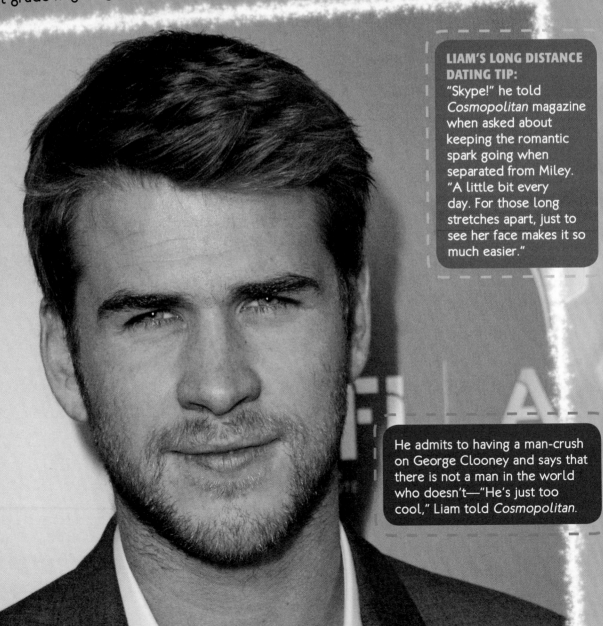

LIAM'S LONG DISTANCE DATING TIP:
"Skype!" he told *Cosmopolitan* magazine when asked about keeping the romantic spark going when separated from Miley. "A little bit every day. For those long stretches apart, just to see her face makes it so much easier."

He admits to having a man-crush on George Clooney and says that there is not a man in the world who doesn't—"He's just too cool," Liam told *Cosmopolitan*.

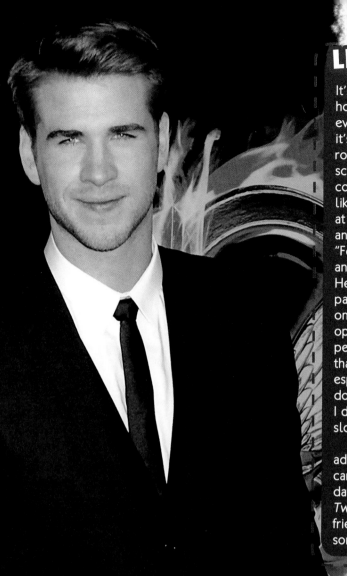

LIAM'S LOVE 101

It's hard to believe that a hottie as nice as Liam could ever be unlucky in love. But it's true. Liam has had some rough sailing on the dating scene. First of all, he doesn't consider himself a smoothie like Gale in *HG*. "I'm not good at talking to girls. I stand there and stare!" he told *seventeen*. "For me, the perfect date is any date that is not awkward." He blames a couple of rocky patches in former relationships on the fact that he tends "to open up too quickly and trust people too much. I've learned that I have to be more careful, especially with people I don't know as well as I think I do. You have to take things slowly—protect your heart."

Cutie Liam has some advice he thinks all singles can apply to meeting and dating successfully. He tells *Twist,* "When you start off as friends it can definitely lead to something else."

ON GETTING MARRIED

"I'm sure I'll get married one day . . . but I'm only 22."
(Details)

liam . . . just sayin'

Here are a few things you might like to know about Liam, straight from the man himself.

ON ACTING WITH AN ACCENT:
"It gets easier and easier. I work with accent coaches a lot and try to do my best to get the Australian out of there. Australians grow up with a lot of American TV; we watch the same movies you watch, so it's not as alien for an Australian to do an American accent as it is for an American to do an Australian accent. You guys don't grow up hearing our accents. It's in the back of your mind, but it's practice, practice, practice." (MTV News)

ON HOW HE PREPPED FOR PLAYING GALE: "I had to lose a lot of weight," Liam told *J-14* magazine. "Gale's poor and doesn't eat a lot because he's trying to provide for his family. I wanted him to look hungry!"

ON HIS CHARACTER, GALE

"As much as [Gale's] against the government and wants to stand up to them, he really is helpless. He can't do anything about it. . . . I just thought it was such a gut-wrenching kind of thought." (*Vanity Fair*)

"My parents and my brothers always taught me to stand up for myself and stay true to myself. That was the biggest thing that Gale and I have in common." (*Justine*)

Liam's TOP 10 TIDBITS

Hope you read our Liam section carefully so that you can score high on this trivia test!

1. Liam encountered a _____ while filming *The Hunger Games*.

2. Liam uses _____ to keep in touch with his GF when they are far apart.

3. Liam describes this Australian dish as, "Pretty much the best thing ever: _____."

4. He began dating Miley Cyrus on the set of _____.

5. He owns up to having a man-crush on fellow actor _____.

6. Miley Cyrus, gave him a cuddly rescue dog named _____.

7. Clean-freak Liam takes multiple _____ every day.

8. For Liam, "The perfect date is any date that is not _____."

9. In order to accurately portray his character Gale in The Hunger Games, Liam had to _____.

10. In first grade Liam had a crush on a girl named Amanda, and admits to treating her more _____ than _____.

LIAM'S NOT-SO-GUILTY SECRET: "I have incredible hygiene," Liam boasted to Moviefone. "I have showers all the time. I smell good!" Well, we're very happy to hear that, Liam! And, we bet, so are your costars!

Answers: 1. black bear; 2. Skype; 3. meat pies; 4. *The Last Song* 5. George Clooney; 6. Ziggy; 7. awkward; 8. brown; 9. lose weight; 10. mean, nice

CRUSH-WORTHY CELEBS

What do you answer when someone asks, "Who is your celebrity crush?" Do you have to think for a minute or can you instantly say, "Justin Bieber!" or "Harry Styles!" or "Cody Simpson!" Well, your favorite SUPERSTARS are just like you—some of them have to take their time before they answer and others know who's crushable right away. Others will only divulge their very first celebrity crush! See how some of Hollywood's hottest have answered that question—but remember, their chick-picks could change before you know it!

zayn malik
"I really fancy Katy Perry! She's beautiful!" (twistmagazine.com)

daniel radcliffe
"I don't love Katy Perry's music, but she's hot," said the *Harry Potter* graduate. "She's my crush!" (M)

corbin bleu
It's Angelina Jolie for the star of the *High School Musical* movies. "I love everything about her. She's fierce, and she's definitely a strong woman, but she's still smart, and kind, and a humanitarian. She's still got that bad girl side to her. Perfect, perfect girl. She's taken, but it's all good." (*seventeen*)

alexander ludwig

"Jessica Alba. I have the biggest crush on her, I can't even tell you. I met her in Vancouver when she was filming *Good Luck Chuck*." (justjaredjr.com)

zac efron

"Growing up, [my celebrity crush] was Tyra Banks. She was the first poster on my wall. I had it on my ceiling! And I had a bunk bed, so she was, like, really close. It was the famous purple bathing suit shot." (anythinghollywood.com)

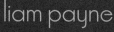

liam payne

"I love a little bit of Miley Cyrus. She's hot!" (twistmagazine.com)

justin bieber

"I would love to take [Emma Watson] out for dinner. I love the fact that she is one of the biggest female movie stars, but has chosen to go back to college. It shows she is really grounded and normal." (cosmopolitan.co.uk)

taylor lautner

"[My crushes have] changed a lot. It used to be Jessica Alba for the longest time, and I'm kind of transferring to Megan Fox." (cosmopolitan.co.uk)

greyson chance

"Scarlett Johansson. Either [her] or Dianna Agron from *Glee*." (Popstar)

logan lerman

"My dream girl is Rachel McAdams. I saw her in a restaurant once and it was the first time I've actually frozen up around a girl. I couldn't even look in the direction of where she was sitting! I'm a huge fan of hers." (justjaredjr.com)

david henrie

"If I could meet Megan Fox, I would . . . probably die. I like her a lot! Sophia Bush is gorgeous. There's a lot. There's so many beautiful girls out here [in L.A.]. It's hard to keep track of them all." *(justjaredjr.com)*

cody simpson

"Selena Gomez. I like her personality—and her looks" *(seventeen.com)*

ryan beatty

"Ariana Grande! She's so talented. She said that I'm a good singer, and that really makes me happy. She's so nice!" *(M)*

sterling knight

"My general cup of tea would be Scarlett Johansson or Natalie Portman—or any of those wonderful people [who] will never talk to me!" *(justjaredjr.com)*

can't get enough of TAYLOR KITSCH

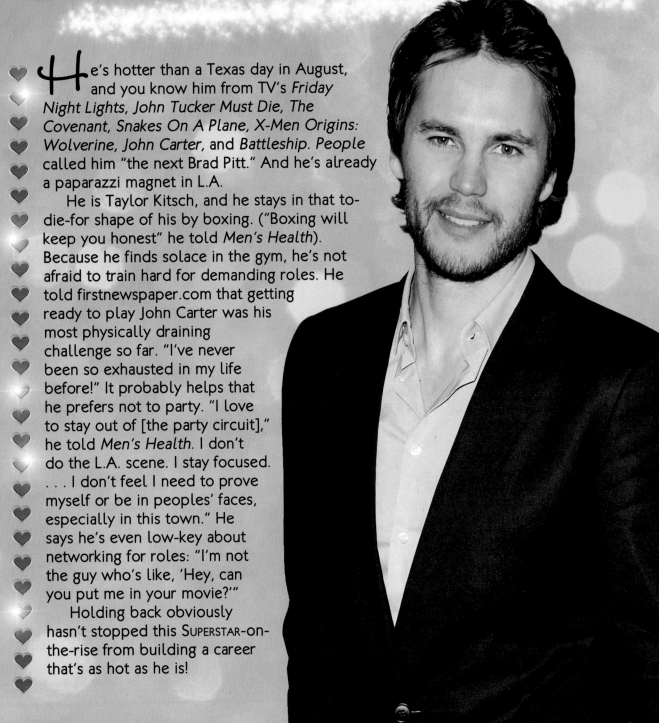

He's hotter than a Texas day in August, and you know him from TV's *Friday Night Lights, John Tucker Must Die, The Covenant, Snakes On A Plane, X-Men Origins: Wolverine, John Carter,* and *Battleship. People* called him "the next Brad Pitt." And he's already a paparazzi magnet in L.A.

He is Taylor Kitsch, and he stays in that to-die-for shape of his by boxing. ("Boxing will keep you honest" he told *Men's Health*). Because he finds solace in the gym, he's not afraid to train hard for demanding roles. He told firstnewspaper.com that getting ready to play John Carter was his most physically draining challenge so far. "I've never been so exhausted in my life before!" It probably helps that he prefers not to party. "I love to stay out of [the party circuit]," he told *Men's Health*. I don't do the L.A. scene. I stay focused. . . . I don't feel I need to prove myself or be in peoples' faces, especially in this town." He says he's even low-key about networking for roles: "I'm not the guy who's like, 'Hey, can you put me in your movie?'"

Holding back obviously hasn't stopped this SUPERSTAR-on-the-rise from building a career that's as hot as he is!

Taylor

taylor—canadian cutie

You can take the boy out of Canada, but you can't take Canada out of the boy! Taylor is the kind of rugged, outdoorsy type who grew up playing hockey and he is one laid-back and grounded dude. He keeps his astounding good looks in perspective—his triceps pop but his head doesn't swell! He even admits that his heart has been broken, and he's not afraid to share his heartaches as well as his joyful moments with fans.

Taylor shies away from the attention usually showered on Hollywood heartthrobs. "It makes you feel weird," he told MTV News. "You get awkward, like I am right now. Hopefully it doesn't turn into validation of self. It is what it is. It's flattering, but at the end of the day, I only have about 6,200 mirrors at my house," he joked. "It's no a big deal. Who doesn't?"

He told *Cosmopolitan* that he is attracted to "a gal who has a great sense of who she is and doesn't need to be with someone all the time." That also entails trust. "With my job, I have to be out of town a lot, so that's huge."

If he could, Taylor would do one thing differently in his love life, he told Scholastic.com. "I had my first date when I was in grade six, I think, and I still regret not kissing her at the end of the night. That was a big thing for me. I freaked out. I was too scared." [laughs]

He likes to keep things low-key when he takes a girl out: "My perfect date is to hang out, laugh, and just have fun. Let things fall with no pressure," he told J-14.

LIFE WASN'T ALWAYS THIS GOOD!

"I've definitely had some interesting experiences," Taylor told firstnewspaper.com. "I didn't just move to Hollywood and immediately become a star. I had to work hard." Though a modeling contract brought him from his native Canada to New York City, he couldn't always afford an apartment, and sometimes had to sleep on friends' couches—or the occasional subway! After moving to L.A. and then to Vancouver, he started picking up acting roles. He still identifies with the "struggling actor" part of his life. "A lot of my friends are non-actors, so that helps a lot, and the actors that I am friends with, they're very similar to what direction I am going in as well. They are more about the work than about celebrity. I like that."

Those close to Taylor know that his take on Hollywood is all his own, but it seems to be serving him well!

taylor trivia

He's funny, he's sexy, he's a talented actor—and he doesn't take himself too seriously, which is definitely an outstanding quality for a heartthrob to have! Though he is quite strict about nutrition and doing strenuous workouts, he says that after getting into shape for certain roles, such as John Carter, he lets himself go for a bit. He admits the first thing he did after completing that role was eat two or three large pizzas! He's human, after all!

HEAD-2-TOE FACT FILE

REAL NAME: Taylor Kitsch

BIRTHDAY: April 8, 1981

BIRTHPLACE: Kelowna, Canada

CURRENT RESIDENCE: Austin, Texas

FIRST JOBS: Model, certified nutritionist and personal trainer

HEIGHT: 6'

FAVORITE ACTOR: Sean Penn

FAVORITE SPORT: Hockey (he played junior league ice hockey in Canada for the Langley Hornets) and wakeboarding

FAVORITE BAND: Pearl Jam (right now, but it changes)

FAVORITE BREAKFAST: Six egg whites with spinach and mushrooms, dry toast, fruit, and coffee

FAVORITE NEW EXTREME SPORT: Cliff-diving (he first tried it while in Hawaii filming *Battleship*)

PERSONAL MOTTO: No regrets

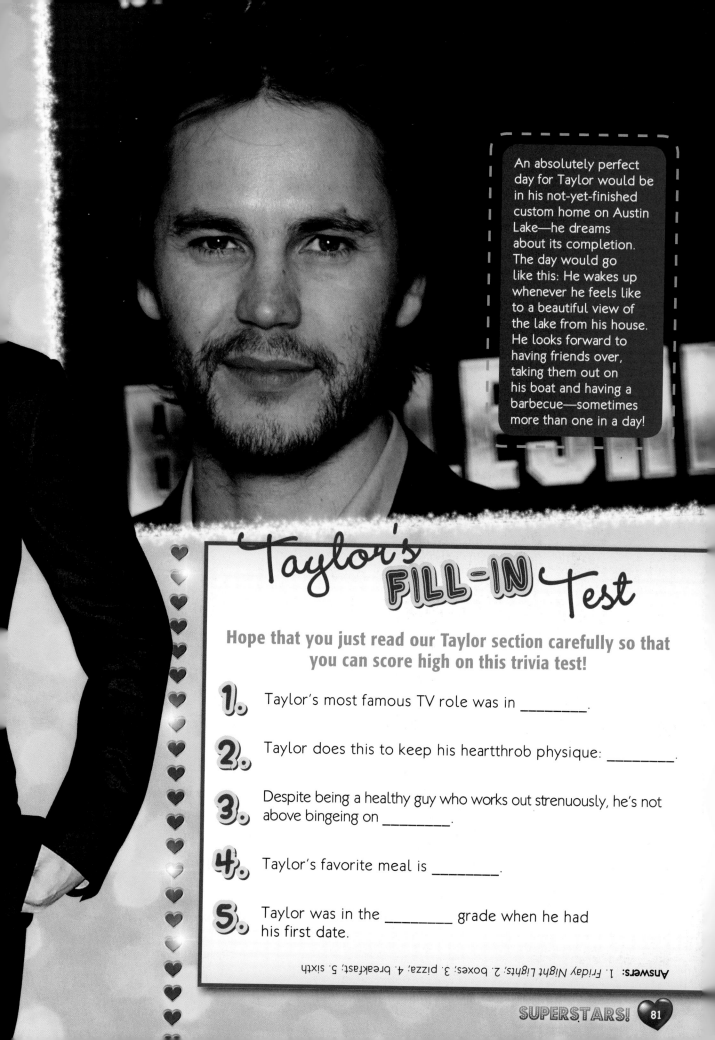

An absolutely perfect day for Taylor would be in his not-yet-finished custom home on Austin Lake—he dreams about its completion. The day would go like this: He wakes up whenever he feels like to a beautiful view of the lake from his house. He looks forward to having friends over, taking them out on his boat and having a barbecue—sometimes more than one in a day!

Taylor's FILL-IN Test

Hope that you just read our Taylor section carefully so that you can score high on this trivia test!

1. Taylor's most famous TV role was in _____.

2. Taylor does this to keep his heartthrob physique: _____.

3. Despite being a healthy guy who works out strenuously, he's not above bingeing on _____.

4. Taylor's favorite meal is _____.

5. Taylor was in the _____ grade when he had his first date.

Answers: 1. Friday Night Lights, 2. boxes, 3. pizza, 4. breakfast, 5. sixth

mad-crazy over ONE DIRECTION

Are you ready for the latest British invasion? Well, you better be because U.K. citizens Harry Styles, Niall Horan, Liam Payne, Zayn Malik, and Louis Tomlinson—better known as One Direction or 1D—have already hit U.S. shores and their quest for world domination is well under way! A tsunami of girls showed up when 1D appeared on the *Today* show in March of 2012, and as the female frenzy spilled over into NYC's midtown streets, even parents stopped in their tracks! Shortly after that performance they dropped their debut album, *Up All Night,* in the U.S. and girls across the country took the title to heart. Hoards of 1D's fans, known as Directioners, camped out all night waiting for the chance to see, hear, and—they could hope!—meet the Fab Five at concert performances or at airports!

With the release of *Up All Night,* 1D became the very first British group to go to No. 1 on the U.S. charts with their first single. Neither the Beatles, nor the Rolling Stones, nor Duran Duran, nor Take That, all mega British imports, achieved that feat! One Direction guest-starred on Nickelodeon's hit show *iCarly*—rumor has it they might be getting their own Nick series, too—and performed at the 2012 Nickelodeon Kids' Choice Awards, where they wowed the audience, including First Lady Michelle Obama and daughters Malia and Sasha, who danced to the guys' "What Makes You Beautiful." They followed that up with an appearance as musical guests on the April 7 *Saturday Night Live*. And they have booked tours around the world into 2013. These guys are going in one direction—up!

One Direction

one direction flirt alert

When you are lucky enough to be around Harry, Liam, Louis, Zayn, and Niall, the subject of romance naturally comes up. While they *do* like to joke around, it turns out they also love to talk about love! After all, that's the subject they sing about to their millions of fans all over the globe. It's close to their hearts.

Of the five, only two have steady girlfriends. Louis has been dating student/model Eleanor Calder and Liam fell for dancer Danielle Peazer when they met on *The X Factor* set. So that leaves Harry, Zayn, and Niall available—and ready, willing, and able—to fall in love. If you're interested in seeing how to catch their attention, read on!

On who is the biggest 1D flirt. . .

LOUIS: "Harry really does flirt with literally EVERY girl!"

NIALL: "I can't compete with Harry's flirting!"

(Bop)

On the perfect girl. . .

ZAYN: "I thought I had a type, but I'm not sure anymore. She just can't take herself too seriously and she's got to be chill, relaxed, and has to like having a laugh. I find that really attractive."

LIAM: "I love a girl who I can spend every day with and genuinely enjoy it. That's important."

NIALL: "I like any girl! [Laughs] If she was a fan, that wouldn't stop me!"

HARRY: "I like girls who make me laugh. Nice people get on with nice people. I just like people who are funny—Not too shy, but sometimes shy is cute."

LOUIS: "I like girls who are adventurous. But most importantly she needs a good smile, must be honest and have a good personality. I also want someone witty!"

(Twist)

On being a good boyfriend. . .

LOUIS: "I'm a bit of a joker. I can be a romantic, but not too sickly—I like to keep it to a level. You have to get the banter in there, too, otherwise you scare the girl away."

NIALL: "I'm nice. I'd treat a girl well and I would buy her presents and take her to nice places. . . . If I really, really like them, then I'm loyal."

HARRY: "I'm very loyal, very faithful, and my mum tells me I'm a romantic. How does she know? Because if she's had a bad day at work, I'll run her a bath and cook her dinner. When I have a girlfriend, I like having someone to spoil. . . . I'm very loyal, but you can look and not touch!"

ZAYN: "I'd like to think I'm caring, considerate, and pretty chilled out. . . . I'm definitely loyal if I've got a girlfriend."

LIAM: "I'd say in One Direction there are a lot of different dynamics— some of the boys are 'Jack the lad' [British for "bad boy"], whereas I'm a bit more of an old romantic. . . . I'm very loyal."

(Teen Now)

1D big reveal

How many facts about One Direction do you already know? Can you hang out with your friends and ace a Directioners trivia fest? Do you know where the guys are from, their birthdays, what their fave lists include, and how they feel about their fans?

Harry, Liam, Louis, Zayn, and Niall recently gave *Bop* some man-to-fan suggestions on how to catch their attention.

ZAYN: "Funny banners and posters with our names on them catch my attention. They make you look twice!"

NIALL: "We love hugging! We have the best fans in the world. We love meeting them."

LIAM: "We love talking to fans."

HARRY: "I would say that when someone meets us, it's nice when they just make conversation."

LOUIS: "Funny tweets are the best. If you're picking through your Twitter and one of the tweets really makes you laugh, that's the one that stands out!"

Test Your 1D I.Q.

You've read through the pages, checked out the photos, and probably picked which 1D guy is your favorite. Now can you take a short quiz and answer some trivia questions? Try!!!!

1. One Direction fans are called _____.

2. The boys of One Direction appeared on what televion show with fellow heartthrob Nathan Kress? _____

3. Which member of One Direction is dating Danielle Peazer? _____

4. Who do the members of One Direction agree is the biggest flirt? _____

5. After the U.S. release of *Up All Night*, One Direction became the first British band to _____.

6. One Direction got to know _____ while opening for them on tour.

7. Which guy has been known to run a bath and cook dinner for his mom when she's had a tough day at work? _____

Answers: 1. Directioners; 2. *iCarly*; 3. Liam; 4. Harry; 5. go to No. 1 on the U.S. charts with their first single; 6. Big Time Rush; 7. Harry

KISSY KISSY LOVE NOTES

First kisses are always special. Your first kiss only comes around once—you'll never experience it again! It could be amazing . . . blush-worthy . . . even a total disaster! But, no matter what, it's special. Share first-kiss memories from some of your favorites—you might giggle or even say "Awwww!"—but you will definitely love their stories.

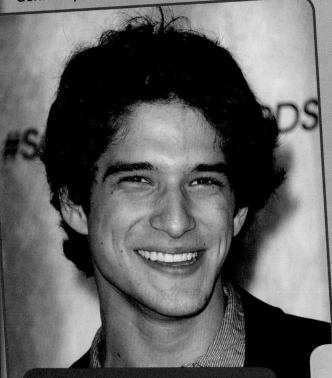

cody simpson

PUCKER UP: "I was in sixth grade, and there was this girl I really liked. We had this theater in our school, and there was a staircase in there that was the place where you'd go when you wanted to give someone a kiss. So we went in there and we're standing there looking at the ground for like 20 minutes. It was awkward for me because I really liked this girl but I didn't know what to do! So then I was like, 'I gotta go.' And then it happened right there! We kissed and after we were just laughing. When we went outside, all my friends were waiting for me! It was pretty cool." (*Twist*)

tyler posey

MILEY SIGH-RUS: Tyler met Miley Cyrus pre-*Hannah Montana* when he worked with her dad on the series *Doc*. It was puppy love at first sight! "She was my first kiss. We dated for two years. I saw her on her on TV three years later and freaked out!" (*J-14*)

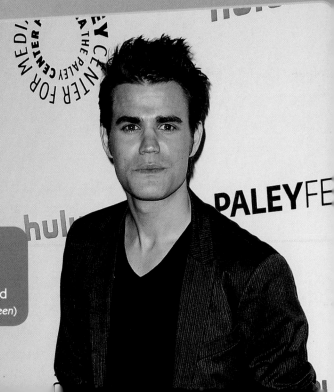

paul wesley

WATER SMOOCH: "I was 9 years old and I was in a swimming pool. There was a girl there, and she dared me or I dared her into kissing me underwater. (*seventeen*)

mitchel musso

KISSES & PB&J: "I had my first kiss in first grade. It was a kiss on the cheek. And it was under a coloring table. I didn't know what was going on, though. I was like, 'Well, well! What do I do now?' Then we went to eat in the lunchroom, and we had our date there. We ate PB&J and chicken fingers." (*Popstar!*)

corbin bleu

FIRST KISS CLUELESS: "[I was] 14. It was around Halloween season at Knott's Berry Farm. I had a crush on her, and it happened on one of the rides, in the dark. I wasn't expecting it at first. I had no idea what I was doing." (*seventeen*)

sterling knight

KISSING IN THE NEW YEAR: "I was at a party on New Year's Eve playing a nice tasteful game of Spin the Bottle. It's hard to not land a kiss while playing that. I know a first kiss on New Year's Eve is a romantic cliché, but I'm from Texas and we love that stuff!" (*M*)

iLove NATHAN KRESS

The show may be known as *iCarly*, but Nathan Kress, the Nick series' dorky-but-lovable Freddie, sometimes even steals the spotlight from Miranda Cosgrove. As the resident brainiac on the show, Freddie often saves the day with one of his tech solutions. In real life, Nathan may not be a brilliant geek, but he shines as one of Hollywood's top teen stars.

When the outspoken Nathan makes an appearance, he loves the give-and-take with fans. He chats easily and answers questions from, "Will Freddie's mother stop treating him like a baby?" to "Will Carly and Freddie ever date again?" Nathan's got the gift for gab for sure, which mesmerizes fans along with his sexy smile and eyes. That spark is what helped him choose acting as a career. From the time he was just 2 or 3 years old, Nathan told missoandfriends.com, "I would memorize stuff from TV and perform it for my family. I was a little performer for most of my early life."

Nathan's parents took him to an audition, which led to print ads, TV commercials, and the voice-over roles of Tough Pup and Easy in the feature film *Babe: Pig in the City*. He loved every minute of it, but by the time Nathan was 6, he had decided to retire and go back to being a normal kid, going to school, hanging with his friends. The only things he memorized were math tables and poems for class assignments!

Then, when he was in fifth grade, Nathan won the role of the Emperor in a school production of *The Emperor's New Clothes*. That rekindled his love of performing and he was back to memorizing dialogue! He quickly went from appearing as the young Simon Cowell in a comedy sketch on *Jimmy Kimmel Live!* to a small role on Nick's top series *Drake & Josh*, and in 2007, Nathan got his biggest break, landing the role of Freddie on Nickelodeon's new show *iCarly*.

Nathan

nathan ... true confession

He may seem confident, but Nathan isn't always that cool when it comes to meeting new girls. Check out the time he says he almost blew it big time!

Nathan was getting ready for a benefit concert at Hollywood's Avalon club when a girl in the crowd caught his eye—and she looked right back at him! "The first 10 minutes we saw each other were incredibly awkward," Nathan told *Bop*. "We kept looking at each other. We both knew we wanted to go up and talk to each other, but we had nothing to talk about."

But Nathan decided he wasn't going to just stand there and let this girl—her name was Madisen Hill—walk away. "It took work to get the conversation going, but at the end of the night, we swapped numbers. I was so happy I got hers."

He was even happier two weeks later when they went out on their first date. And more than two years later, they were still going strong!

> Nathan told *Bop*, "I'm an outdoorsy guy. I like to go camping and fishing. I'd like a girl who's into that stuff, too."

Nathan and Madisen Hill

Nathan likes a date out in nature. "I'm a fishing, hiking, and camping guy," he told *Bop*. "I would definitely take my date to do something active! For girls who are not outdoorsy, I would make a picnic dinner." That would include making s'mores over a grill or a campfire.

NATHAN'S DOs & DONTs OF DATING

Nathan is an open-minded dater but he does have some serious turn-ons and turn-offs.

Don't wear heavy fragrance! He said to *Bop*, "I like subtle scents, not perfume fumigating off as someone walks by."

Don't pursue him—he's old-fashioned in that way! He said to *Tiger Beat*, "I don't want girls chasing me. I want to start the relationship and be the gentleman."

Do love Disneyland or Disney World. Nathan says he took Madisen for their Valentine's Day date to a café in Disneyland's Downtown Disney District—they mixed and matched menu items and enjoyed combining gourmet grub with comfort food!

Do be laid back and go with the flow on a date with Nathan. He's turned off when date activities are too planned out.

He likes girls who look chic without showing a lot of skin—and have their own style!

Do like roses. They're his fave type of flower to send girls.

Nathan likes a girl with sea legs. He told *Bop*, "It's so peaceful when you are outside or in a boat with your friends and family, drinking root beer! It's really relaxing and energizing at the same time!"

all about nathan

He's a guy who loves his dog and The *Lord of the Rings* trilogy and has a crush on Keira Knightley. Nate says he's grateful for the opportunity to learn more and more each day—and to meet new people!

He was home-schooled from sixth grade onward.

He's not a fan of high heels. He said to *seventeen*, "It definitely confuses the heck out of me. With all the complaints about how painful and impractical they are, why do women still wear them? And it doesn't help that I'm not very tall, so it makes even the shorter girls taller than me. Not cool!"

If he could trade places with anyone for one day, it would be the President. Is that because he wants to lead the country—or hang out with First Lady Michelle?

He puts peanut butter on his hot dogs! He told *Twist*, "It's absolutely delicious! One of my friends became a peanut butter-hot dog convert recently. He said he was nervous to try it and then he did it. He loved it; he woofed it down!"

Miranda Cosgrove and Nathan

¡Quiz ON AN iHunk

Will you pass? Well, Nathan loves Twitter more than any other social media, so you could always ask him for the answers in a tweet, LOL!

1. Nathan stopped going to public school after:

A) Fourth grade   C) Sixth grade

B) Fifth grade   D) Seventh grade

2. Nathan's favorite condiment for hot dogs is:

A) Mustard   C) Mayonnaise

B) Ketchup   D) Peanut butter

3. He spent this past Valentine's Day at:

A) Disneyland   C) Disney World

B) Knott's Berry Farm   D) Six Flags Great Adventure

4. Nathan thinks it's ridiculous when women wear:

A) Lipstick   C) Hats

B) High heels   D) Hoodies

5. Nathan's celebrity crush is:

A) Miley Cyrus   C) Keira Knightley

B) Rihanna   D) Katy Perry

6. Nathan would be most turned off by the potential date-mate who:

A) Makes the first move   C) Likes to play Xbox 360

B) Likes to fish and camp   D) Wears a subtle fragrance

Answers: 1. B—fifth grade; 2. D—peanut butter; 3. A—Disneyland; 4. B—high heels; 5. C—Keira Knightley; 6. A—makes the first move.

crazy over CODY

Cody Simpsons's long-awaited debut CD, *Paradise*, is due in June 2012 and fans couldn't be more excited: The boy who is a bit of thunder from Down Under is rumbling across the U.S. and Canada on tour throughout the summer!

Yeah, mate, Cody-Mania is thicker than Vegemite, and spreading faster than a speeding kangaroo. This Aussie moved to L.A. in 2010 to pursue his career, but still travels back to his homeland to see family and friends twice a year just to stay grounded. To quote one of his song titles, his fans are always "on his mind" no matter where he is in the world!

Cody

incredibly cute cody!

This Aussie doesn't have a GF; he says it's hard to have a relationship when you travel all the time. But for the record, he likes girls who are kind, funny, and quirky. Does that describe you? Here's the scoop on how to get his baby blues to wink at YOU!

5 DATE-MATE DO'S

1 Do try to date in your age group—Cody knows this from personal experience. He tells *J-14*, "I once had a big crush on a girl who was a few years older than me. I was 10 and she was 13. I was totally in love with her, but it didn't work out. I think if you're more than two years older, that's pushing the limit a little."

Cody fantasizes about meeting his dream girl just as much as you dream about meeting HIM! He has even written a song, "Love So Strong," about a girl he really liked! He told *Twist* that they had to break up because he was leaving the country. He also said that he likes a girl "who can be herself around me . . . who's honest, kind, and can make me laugh." And listen to this, girls: Cody is even open to dating a fan! "Definitely!" he told *J-14*. "Anything can happen!"

2 Do find someone to talk to if your guy breaks up with you. Cody tells *J-14,* "I have a few good friends who are girls. If one of them is ever getting treated badly by a guy, I always explain to her, 'Don't cry your heart out because I'm here for you.' They can always trust me."

3 Do take your time. Don't rush into a relationship because sometimes you can make a big mistake if you're only going on that crushin' feeling. "I want to make sure I really get to know a girl when I like her," Cody told *Tiger Beat.* "I flirt, but I take things slow. I don't want to rush anything."

4 Do use your sense of humor to talk to your crush. Cody thinks people are more relaxed and can be themselves when they are having a laugh—even if they have a beet red face from an embarrassing moment. He says, "I love girls who are funny and can make me laugh."

5 Do try to talk to or ask out a guy that you like. Cody thinks it's okay to make friendly chat with guys in order to feel them out and says it is okay to even ask guys out.

1, 2, 3's of cody

Cody tries to eat a healthy diet and stick to a regime that keeps his voice in fine form for concerts. He considers friends and family more important than career, though—and likes to think of his fans as old friends! Want more Cody must-know-info? Read on!

"Every night before I perform," Cody told *Bop*, "I drink chamomile tea. It's good for my voice."

He also loves country music. "I'm a big Taylor Swift fan. I think her music is really great," he told *Tiger Beat*.

Cody confesses to an obsession with *Harry Potter!*

Cody goes to his parents when he needs advice. "My mom and dad have been through everything—they know the most," he told *Tiger Beat*.

Cody was once mistaken for Cody Linley, who played Miley Cyrus's off-and-on boyfriend on her longstanding Disney Channel series *Hannah Montana*.

Selena Gomez recently came up to Cody and said that she was a fan!

Cody's Life IN PARADISE

This is a true brain-teaser—you HAVE to be a real Cody fan because the answers are NOT in the previous pages!

Fill in the blanks on the babe from Down Under!

1. Like a lot of teenage boys, Cody puts what condiment on nearly all his food? _____.

2. Cody has two siblings; one is his sister Alli and one is his brother _____.

3. Cody plays the acoustic guitar at every show, but what new instrument has he been learning? _____.

4. Cody's wish for a superpower would be the ability to _____.

5. Cody says the lady he texts most is _____.

6. When Cody has a crush on a girl, the first physical feature he notices is _____.

7. Cody's bespectacled dad's name is _____.

8. Cody can speak a second language; it's _____.

9. Cody's Twitter handle is _____.

10. Like Liam Hemsworth, Cody is obsessed with collecting _____.

Answers: 1. ketchup; 2. Tom; 3. piano; 4. to fly; 5. his mom; 6. her eyes; 7. Brad; 8. French; 9. @simpsoncody; 10. shoes.

SEXY SUPERNATURALS

What is it about fangs, magic spells, and suddenly sprouting body hair that we find so alluring? Vampires, witches, werewolves, and other supernatural beings have invaded the hottie space, turning up the temperature to inferno levels! On TV, there have been *The Secret Circle, The Vampire Diaries, Teen Wolf, Supernatural, Fringe, Touch,* and more. Perhaps it was the The *Twilight* Saga series that started it all, and now we have *Dark Shadows* too. Our fascination with otherworldy creatures seems to be. . . immortal! Here are some of the spookily appealing characters on our screens and the actors who have such fun playing them.

Thomas Dekker's *The Secret Circle* character, Adam, definitely has otherworldly appeal as a boy-next-door witch who can use his powers for good or evil. He chooses good, but he could turn you into a bug, an animal, or a statue if he wanted! EEK!

Thomas told collider.com that what he likes about his character is that he's very aware of how to control his abilities. "Most of the other kids are completely out of control with it. He takes pleasure in the small things, like getting a pencil to stand upright, or getting a chair to move. He starts slowly, whereas the other ones are like, 'Hey, let's start a lightning storm.' I like his grace and his control."

thomas mcdonell

Way back before your time, in the late 1960s and early 1970s, kids ran home after school to watch the first supernatural TV soap opera, *Dark Shadows*. The vampire, Barnabas Collins, was the Edward Cullen of his day! Today, Thomas McDonell is the young version of Johnny Depp's Barnabas Collins in the 2012 film update of the iconic soap opera. Before the movie *Dark Shadows* was released, Thomas told *Movieline* that he was excited about the role, but "I didn't know much about *Dark Shadows*. And I had certainly not watched any of it. But the more I'm learning all the time, the weirder and more interesting I think the film could be."

You might recognize Thomas from *Prom*—he played Jesse. He caught the acting bug in China! "I studied art in school and I got my first job working on a film sort of as an experiment when I was living and studying contemporary art in China," he told *Movieline*. "I went on an audition and got a part in a kung fu film there."

ian somerhalder

Twilight's Edward Cullen was sexy from the get-go, and he's still going strong with the scheduled release of *Breaking Dawn Part 2* in November 2012. But did you know that Ian Somerhalder's Damon of *The Vampire Diaries* beat him out in a fang-to-fang battle? Damon was voted the "Ultimate Sexy Beast" in an *Entertainment Weekly* poll in 2010—he beat Edward in a final vote of 138,630 to 134,728.

Ian loves playing a character who's of the living-dead persuasion, but in real life would he choose the ultimate bite? "Two things just to contemplate for two seconds," he told TVNX. com. "Immortality: everything you've ever known, everyone you've ever known dies. And on top of that, being a vampire, how long it would take to curb every sense you have. The five senses. . . now multiply them times a thousand." Umm. . . is that a yes or a no?

paul wesley

When *The Vampire Diaries* first started, Paul Wesley's character Stefan was the "good" vampire, the fanger who refused to harm a human, the biter who fell in love with the living, breathing Elena. In the 2012 season, things changed and he reverted to the evil ways he'd abandoned in the past. Paul says he not only enjoyed playing the other side of Stefan, he also liked the fact that female fans seemed to prefer him that way. "I'm thinkin' to myself, it's so funny, you'd think the girls would enjoy the good guy, the hero, the protagonist," he told *Entertainment Weekly*. "But it's like, no, that's why nice guys finish last. [Laughs] It's really true. And as an actor, it's just so much more enjoyable."

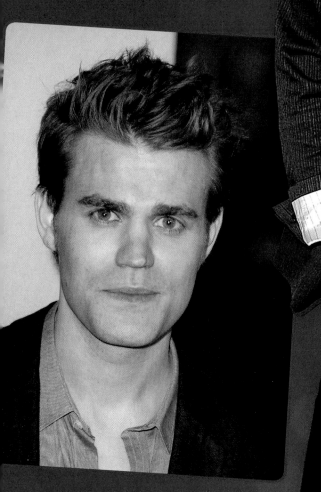

DIGGY SIMMONS
...dig it!

$\mathcal{W}$e first saw Diggy as a 10-year-old on the MTV reality show *Run's House* starring with his dad, Rev. Run Simmons of Run-DMC, mom Justine, and five siblings: Angela, Vanessa, JoJo, Russy, and Miley. On the series, which ran from 2005 to 2009, we got to see Diggy's interest in music grow, but no one suspected that it was going to be so important to him—not even his dad!

Diggy started writing his own raps, doing mix-tapes, and performing all on his own in 2009. "I could have been a doctor. I could have been a lawyer," Diggy told the *Washington Post*. "It's not because of my family that I [rap]. I do it because I love it. I was always able to rap. I used to do musicals in school. I just love to perform in general. I started rapping when I was 5 'til like the age of 8 and then I swayed away from it, and then I had no choice but to get back into it. And nobody knew, not my dad, not my mom, not my brothers or sisters or anybody. It was just me writing."

When Rev. Run heard Diggy's first mix-tape, *The First Flight*, it was a big surprise—and he was super shocked when things exploded from there. "He's so proud of me because so much has come up with me doing my own thing by myself," Diggy told *Vibe*. "He barely even knew what I was doing. . . [he] didn't hear the mix-tape until two weeks after [it was finished and on the Internet]. He was astonished."

Billboard named Diggy one of 2011's Artists To Watch and the same year he joined the Scream Tour with Mindless Behavior, Jacob Latimore, the OMG Girlz, and others. On March 20, 2012, the day before his 17th birthday, he gave himself the best present ever: He released his debut album. And shortly after that he started his own Life of the Jetsetter Tour!

Diggy

diggy in love

Diggy Simmons is definitely easy on the eyes, but he's also talented, smart, a joker, and he's lots of fun. While he could easily be part of the bling-set, he says he's not into the flash and dash of showbiz. He's looking for someone who is interested in him just for who he is, not what he is! Though he's been nicknamed the Jetsetter General and does get to travel the world, he prefers to be a homebody. When he's not working, he would much rather hang out with his family and friends—and that includes the girl he might be dating at the time. It's really important to Diggy that every romantic relationship starts with a solid friendship.

MEANING OF LOVE: "Love is a feeling and something that is unconditional that you have for a person . . . the care for them," Diggy told vibe.com. "And really, like, you would do anything for them to be happy and comfort them."

FIRST DATE: "It may seem cliché, but there's nothing wrong with bowling or movies or dinner or anything like that," Diggy told hellobeautiful.com. "I also like to do fun stuff too, like, we could go to the beach…I'd just think of different things that could just be fun for us and at the same time just be able to get to know each other better, just communicate."

DREAM GIRL QUALITIES: "Definitely somebody with self-respect," he told divawhispers.com. "Somebody I can be compatible with. Somebody that can be themselves around me. I can be myself around her. And you know, just mesh well together, have a good time."

BEAUTY: "I just love a girl [who's] beautiful not only on the outside but the inside too," rapper Diggy told *Jet*. "I don't want anybody [who's] mean or cold. I want somebody [who] is great to be around, a real sweetheart.

FATHERLY LOVE ADVICE: "Honestly, he really just steps back and lets me do a lot of that stuff. . . if I were to ever go to him, of course, he'll help me, but he really lets me figure out that stuff on my own." (divawhispers.com)

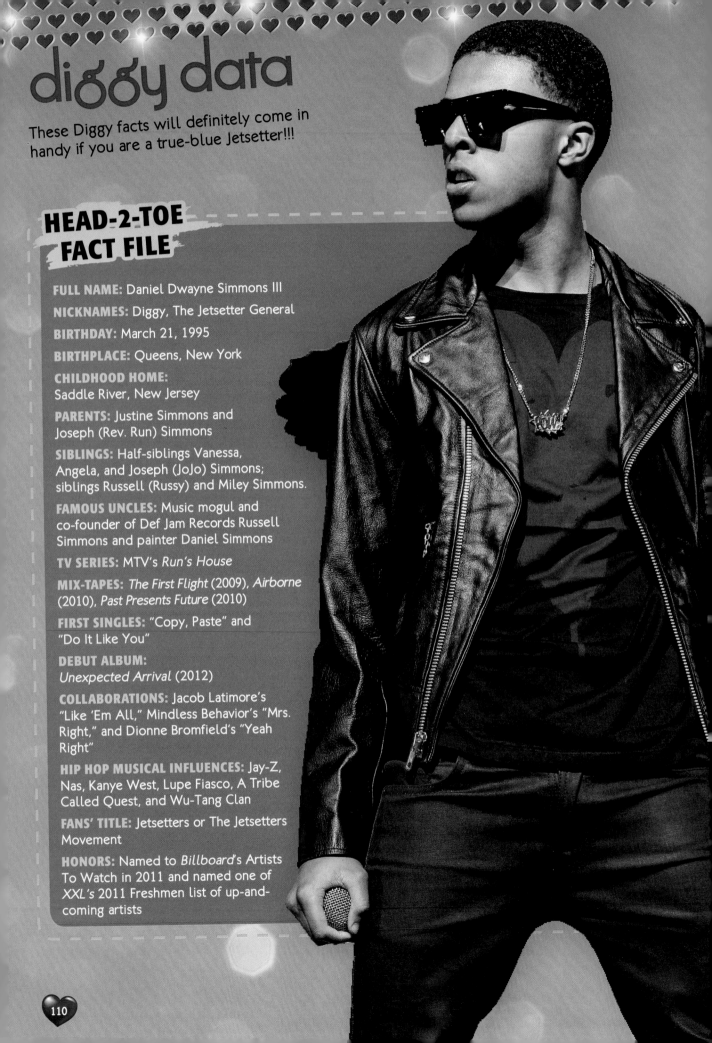

diggy data

These Diggy facts will definitely come in handy if you are a true-blue Jetsetter!!!

HEAD-2-TOE FACT FILE

FULL NAME: Daniel Dwayne Simmons III

NICKNAMES: Diggy, The Jetsetter General

BIRTHDAY: March 21, 1995

BIRTHPLACE: Queens, New York

CHILDHOOD HOME:
Saddle River, New Jersey

PARENTS: Justine Simmons and Joseph (Rev. Run) Simmons

SIBLINGS: Half-siblings Vanessa, Angela, and Joseph (JoJo) Simmons; siblings Russell (Russy) and Miley Simmons.

FAMOUS UNCLES: Music mogul and co-founder of Def Jam Records Russell Simmons and painter Daniel Simmons

TV SERIES: MTV's *Run's House*

MIX-TAPES: *The First Flight* (2009), *Airborne* (2010), *Past Presents Future* (2010)

FIRST SINGLES: "Copy, Paste" and "Do It Like You"

DEBUT ALBUM:
Unexpected Arrival (2012)

COLLABORATIONS: Jacob Latimore's "Like 'Em All," Mindless Behavior's "Mrs. Right," and Dionne Bromfield's "Yeah Right"

HIP HOP MUSICAL INFLUENCES: Jay-Z, Nas, Kanye West, Lupe Fiasco, A Tribe Called Quest, and Wu-Tang Clan

FANS' TITLE: Jetsetters or The Jetsetters Movement

HONORS: Named to *Billboard*'s Artists To Watch in 2011 and named one of *XXL*'s 2011 Freshmen list of up-and-coming artists

SCRAMBLED Diggy

Below are five words or names you've read here about Diggy. The letters have been jumbled up— see if you can unscramble them.

1. TTTJEEESRS
(HINT: Another name for Diggy's fans)

2. ELUP SCOFIA
(HINT: He's one of Diggy's role models)

3. SNUR SHOEU
(HINT: The family's MTV reality show)

4. FLES-PSREECT
(HINT: The quality Diggy most looks for in a girl)

5. PETEDEUNX VIRARLA
(HINT: Diggy's debut)

Answers: 1. JETSETTERS, 2. LUPE FIASCO, 3. RUN'S HOUSE, 4. SELF-RESPECT, 5. UNEXPECTED ARRIVAL.

NOT FROM AROUND HERE

There is something so charming about accents and local expressions. How many times have you asked a friend or family member from another country to pronounce a specific word or use a certain phrase? It's so cute when a Canadian says "oot" instead of "out," or when a Brit calls "sneakers" "trainers," or an Aussie says "G'day" instead of "Hello." (And hopefully, Canadians and Brits and Aussies find some things we say, and the way we say them, charming too!) Of course, accents and local-speak are just a small part of why we love the following heartthrobs, and just part of where they come from. Let's find out more about the foreign lands these cute-talking boys call home, and then see if you can answer the questions from our quiz.

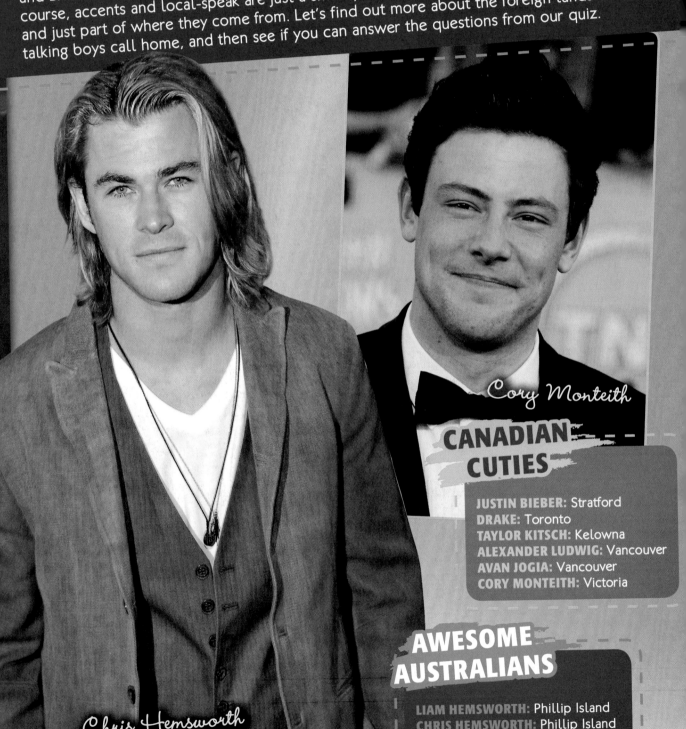

Cory Monteith

Chris Hemsworth

CANADIAN CUTIES

JUSTIN BIEBER: Stratford
DRAKE: Toronto
TAYLOR KITSCH: Kelowna
ALEXANDER LUDWIG: Vancouver
AVAN JOGIA: Vancouver
CORY MONTEITH: Victoria

AWESOME AUSTRALIANS

LIAM HEMSWORTH: Phillip Island
CHRIS HEMSWORTH: Phillip Island
CODY SIMPSON: Gold Coast
JORDAN JANSEN: Gold Coast

Louis Tomlinson
Liam Payne
Zayn Malik
Niall Horan
Harry Styles
One Direction

UNITED KINGDOM IDOLS

ONE DIRECTION
HARRY STYLES: Holmes Chapel, England
NIALL HORAN: Mullingar, Ireland
LIAM PAYNE: Wolverhampton. England
ZAYN MALIK: Bradford, England
LOUIS TOMLINSON: Doncaster, England

THE WANTED
MAX GEORGE: Manchester, England
JAY MCGUINESS: Newark, England
SIVA KANESWARAN: Arva, Ireland
TOM PARKER: Bolton, England
NATHAN SYKES: Abbeydale, England

DANIEL RADCLIFFE: London, England
ROBERT PATTINSON: London, England
JAMIE CAMPBELL BOWER: London, England
GREGG SULKIN: London, England

FREQUENT FLYER Quiz

Test your knowledge of your favorites' homelands!

1. What is the national animal of Cody Simpson's native Australia?
_____

2. When you are in Gregg Sulkin's hometown, London, what is the biggest clock for all to see?
_____

3. The Wanted's Max George is from Manchester, England. What is the name of its famous soccer team?
_____

4. What famous athletic event took place in Avan Jogia's hometown of Vancouver in 2010? _____

5. The Wanted's Siva Kaneswaran is from Ireland. What is his homeland's nickname?_____

Answers: 1) Kangaroo; 2) Big Ben on the Palace of Westminster; 3) Manchester United Football Club; 4) 2010 Winter Olympics; 5) The Emerald Isle.

OMG! MOMENTS

You know when you are trying to impress that special someone? Succeed, and you feel as if you will never forget the experience. Memories of your first prom or first summer love can feel like that. And then there are the disasters, those embarrassing moments that make even bigger impressions—those you wish you'd forget!

But with time, even the worst embarrassment can be an ice-breaker or a funny tale to tell when you want to make your new love laugh! Believe it or not, your favorites have their share of OMG! traumas too. Bet you will get a giggle or two after checking these out!

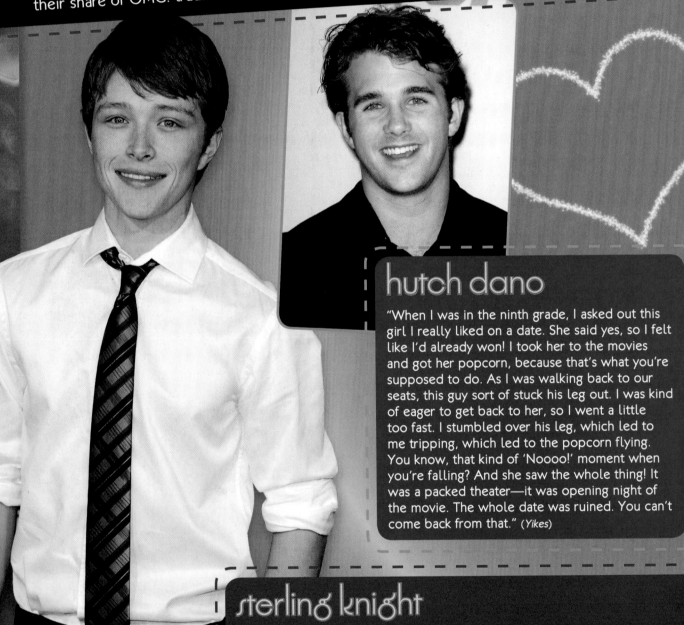

hutch dano

"When I was in the ninth grade, I asked out this girl I really liked on a date. She said yes, so I felt like I'd already won! I took her to the movies and got her popcorn, because that's what you're supposed to do. As I was walking back to our seats, this guy sort of stuck his leg out. I was kind of eager to get back to her, so I went a little too fast. I stumbled over his leg, which led to me tripping, which led to the popcorn flying. You know, that kind of 'Noooo!' moment when you're falling? And she saw the whole thing! It was a packed theater—it was opening night of the movie. The whole date was ruined. You can't come back from that." *(Yikes)*

sterling knight

"My parents will bring out the naked baby photos at the drop of a hat. They really don't shy away from any opportunity to make my face turn bright red. I went out on a date with this girl, and I brought her over to meet my parents for a minute to say hello. My mom said, 'Let me show you these pictures!' Out comes the green album. I said, 'Mom, come on! Put them down!'" *(Yikes)*

lucas till

"I was so stupid in a relationship. I said things to a family member about my [girlfriend at the time], but when she heard what I said, it was exaggerated. She took everything the wrong way and got mad!... I didn't know how to deal with the situation and I ended up saying some stupid things. I suffered for it—my heart was broken." (M)

david henrie

"I'm a little lactose intolerant sometimes, and we just had yogurt. Let's just say, it got really stinky, really fast! And she knew it wasn't her. It was really embarrassing, but I made fun of myself." (J-14)

zac efron

"I had a kissing scene one time and I ate a tuna sandwich [for lunch] and I got called out on it. It was so embarrassing. . . . You don't do that, don't be that guy!" (yahoo.com)

FUN IN THE SUN

Whether it's a Fourth of July barbecue and fireworks display, an annual family vacation to the mountains or shore, or first crushes at summer camp, those magical months of June, July, and August make for life-long memories! It starts the moment the school bell rings for the final time and kids spill out of the building, ready for their summer adventures. And then it circles around to the first English class assignment in September—write an essay about "What I did this summer!" Well, guess what—you have those memories (and fantasies!) and so do your favorite SUPERSTARS. Check out some of their fun-in-the-sun times!

lucas till

The *X-Men: First Class* actor says, "I speak German—I took it in school. I went on a [summer] exchange trip to Germany and I loved it. I was there for three weeks. We went to Berlin and Dresden." (*PopStar*)

tyler james williams

The ultimate summer vacation for *Let It Shine*'s star Tyler would be on the court! "[I would like] a camp where I could play basketball 24 hours a day." (*Nickelodeon*)

MITCHEL MUSSO

"I used to go to church camp for the summer [back home] in Texas. I only went until fifth grade and then I was just over camp!" (*Tiger Beat*)

josh hutcherson

"We had these giant neighborhood block parties," [in Union, Kentucky]. "Everyone would bring lots of food and drinks and we'd eat all day. We'd have a fireworks show. I always enjoyed that—it's my fondest summer memory." (*Twist*)

kevin jonas

"I went to camp in Pennsylvania. It's awesome. Going to camp, meeting a girl, and that's all you think about the entire time—and then you go and you never see her again." (*Tiger Beat*)

TYLER BLACKBURN

"I went to summer sleep-away camp. There was a girl there when I was 12 that I liked and we had a five-day fling. One time some of us guys went over to the girls' side late at night! But mainly we would see each other at dinner or at night by the campfire." (*Twist*)

nathan kress

"Somewhere I've definitely always wanted to go is Hawaii. It's always kind of been a dream to be able to do that as a family and either go on a cruise there or just take a plane there and just sit out by the beach and relax!" (*PopStar*)

SUPER IDENTITY

Josh Hutcherson . . . Zac Efron . . . Justin Bieber —they may be SUPERSTARS in their own right, but, boys being boys, they've also fantasized about being superheroes and having fantastic superpowers. Check out your favorite guys' favorite superheroes—and the superpowers they'd order up if they could.

ZAC EFRON
Superhero: Spider-Man and the
Teenage Mutant Ninja Turtles' Raphael
"[When I was little] I asked my mom to specifically get the underwear with Raphael on it. I really loved it." (*People*)

ROBBIE AMELL:
Favorite Superhero: Spider-Man

NATHAN KRESS:
Wish-List Superpower: A mix of teleportation and flight

REED ALEXANDER:
Favorite Superhero: Spider-Man

JAKE T. AUSTIN:
Wish-List Superpower: Flying

LOGAN HENDERSON:
Favorite Superhero: Batman

ROBERT PATTINSON:
Favorite Superheroes: Spider-Man
and *X-Men's* Gambit

JOSH HUTCHERSON:
Favorite Superhero: Batman

JAKE SHORT:
Favorite Superhero: Batman
Wish-List Superpower: Invisibility

spencer boldman

WISH-LIST SUPERPOWER: To fly—
"I think I would conquer my fear of heights quickly!" (seventeen.com)

JUSTIN BIEBER
Superhero: Captain America
"My favorite definitely has to be Captain America. I know that sounds weird because I'm Canadian, but I actually love Captain America and everything he stands for." (comicbookmovie.com)

booboo stewart

FAVORITE SUPERHERO: "My favorite is Nightcrawler, but I wouldn't want to be him. He has a pretty hard life. I'd want to be one that looked normal, but had a really cool power. I'd want to be Superman." (the-trades.com)

JOE JONAS
Superhero: Spider-Man and Underwear Man
"For the longest time I put underwear over my head and ran around the house with my brothers saying, 'I'm the Underwear Man!'" (People)

billy unger

WISH-LIST SUPERPOWER: "I would want my sense of taste to be better. Just so I could taste things that other people couldn't. It's kind of goofy, but that could be cool. . . . I'd want to be super intelligent though, for sure." (disneyinfonet.com)

TAYLOR LAUTNER
Superhero: Spider-Man
Because "he's really cool in the movies." (movieweb.com)

BIG & SMALL SCREEN FAVES

Check and see if your favorite movies or favorite TV shows match up with your celebrity faves' picks! And then take the Quick Quiz to see if you can identify facts about those big and small screen-viewing delights. Good luck!

austin butler

"I watched *Singin' in the Rain* for the first time when I was really young. It just makes me so happy." (*GL*)

paul wesley

". . . *The Goonies* or one of *The Godfather* movies. I'm a sucker for . . . reruns. Anytime they're on, I can't leave the house. I know exactly what's going to happen, and I'm still riveted." (*seventeen*)

Robert Downey Jr.

taylor lautner

"It pulled so many different emotions out of me, so I would have to go with *Braveheart*." (reelz.com)

Robert Downey Jr.

BIG SCREEN FAVES

AVAN JOGIA: *Taxi Driver, Benny & Joon, Amélie*

DILLON LANE: *A Knight's Tale*

JAKE SHORT: *Star Wars*

SPENCER BOLDMAN: *Butch Cassidy and the Sundance Kid, Roman Holiday, Cool Hand Luke*

CODY SIMPSON: [Childhood movie] *Aladdin*

thomas dekker

"I am obsessed with horror movies, so it's nearly impossible for me to pick one. However ... I'd say the best one to get you and a group of friends in the mood [for Halloween] is the brilliantly executed *Poltergeist*. I first saw it when I was about 8 years old, and it absolutely terrified me." (MTV News)

SMALL SCREEN FAVES

CODY SIMPSON: *The Mentalist*

JAKE SHORT: *Parks and Recreation*

SPENCER BOLDMAN: *Modern Family*

MITCHEL MUSSO: *American Idol*

DYLAN SPROUSE: *American Chopper*

TAYLOR LAUTNER: *American Idol* and *Dog, The Bounty Hunter*

CORBIN BLEU: *SpongeBob SquarePants*

GLENN MCCUEN: *The X Factor*

SIVA KANESWARAN: *Family Guy*

RYAN POTTER: "I loved *Heroes* when it was on! George Takei [my co-star on *Supah Ninjas*] was on that. *SpongeBob SquarePants* is still one of my all-time favorite shows." *(Pixie)*

logan miller

"I really like watching cooking shows, like *Ace of Cakes*." *(Yikes!)*

jason dolley

"*Wipeout*—it is one of the funniest shows I've ever seen. People compete for $50,000, but they [have] to do these ridiculous obstacle courses. It's based on Japanese game shows." *(Pixie)*

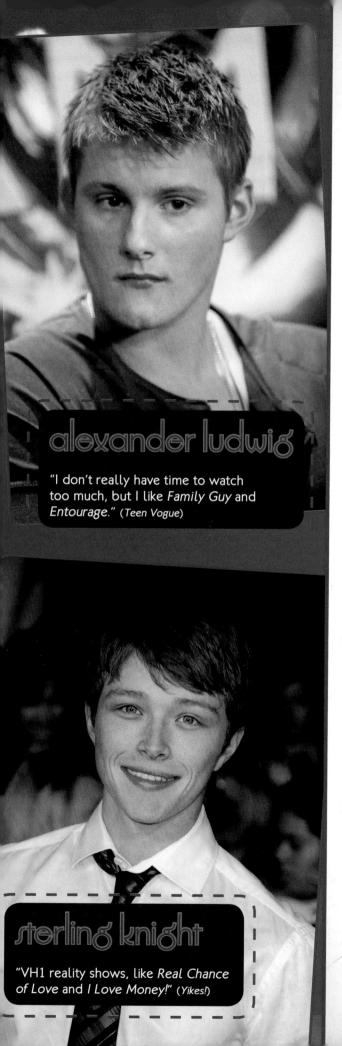

alexander ludwig

"I don't really have time to watch too much, but I like *Family Guy* and *Entourage*." (*Teen Vogue*)

sterling knight

"VH1 reality shows, like *Real Chance of Love* and *I Love Money!*" (*Yikes!*)

Quick Quiz

1. Who were the judges on *The X Factor* in 2011?

A) Paula Adbul, Simon Cowell, Babyface, Nicole Scherzinger

B) Adam Levine, Cee Lo Green, Christina Aguilera, Blake Shelton

C) Carrie Ann Inaba, Bruno Tonioli, Len Goodman

2. The movie *The Goonies* starred Josh Brolin and Sean Astin. Do you know what year it came out?

A) 1995

B) 1963

C) 1985

3. Taylor Lautner's favorite movie, *Braveheart*, is about a famous real-life leader during the 13th century. What country was he from?

A) Ireland

B) England

C) Scotland

4. BTR's Logan Miller never misses *Ace of Cakes*. It's a reality show set in the Baltimore bakery, Charm City Cakes. On which network does it appear?

A) Bravo

B) Food Network

C) Lifetime

5. *Bucket & Skinner's* Dillon Lane says *A Knight's Tale* is his all-time favorite movie. Do you know what classic epic it was based on? [Hint: It was written in the Middle Ages.]

A) *The Canterbury Tales*

B) *The Odyssey*

C) *Romeo and Juliet*

Answers: 1. (a); 2 (c); 3 (c); 4 (b); 5 (a).

PICK YOUR HEARTTHROB

Which one—or two or three—of the cutie-pie celebrities on these pages are you crushin' on? Justin Bieber? Diggy Simmons? 1D's Harry Styles? Cody Simpson? All of the BTR boys? You've devoured the deets about them in this book—now it's time for you to decide which hottie is the SUPERSTAR of your dreams.

You may already think you know who you want. But are you basing that on the way he looks or the way he sounds when he's singing and seems to be serenading you and only you? Well, what about this: What does he say about girls and love and relationships? We think that's a real clue to picking the kind of guy you'd like whispering sweet nothings in your ear!

On this spread and the next one are quotes from 12 of the heartthrobs in this book. Their comments are all about what they like to do on dates and what attracts them to that special girl. Read them and pick which quote really speaks to you. Then see if you can match it up with the sigh-guys listed. Is he the one you had in mind for the role of your own personal heartthrob? Or is he someone you hadn't considered? Or—is it too hard to choose just one?

Josh Hutcherson

Harry Styles

Spencer Boldman

A "You don't have to spend a lot of money on a date all the time. One thing I love doing is, if you're just chilling, or watching a movie, be like, 'Yo, get dressed, come with me, let's go for a walk.' Then take her for a walk. Girls like when you do spontaneous things." (*Twist*)

B "I like being friends first before getting into a relationship. Then the awkwardness is gone!" (*Tiger Beat*)

C "I really like relaxed, comfortable, nice dinners . . . or a picnic at the beach, something like that. Somewhere you can talk, laugh and have fun." (lenalamoray.com)

D Girlfriend must-have qualities: She should: "1. have a sense of humor; 2. be spontaneous; and 3. be a good cook. (I love to eat!)" (fanquarterly.com)

Taylor Lautner

James Maslow

Nathan Kress

E "[I like] someone who can be a dork. I don't want anybody too uptight and trying to impress me. If they're just outgoing and fun, then that works for me." *(GL)*

F "I like feisty girls who can really hang with guys. . . . She's got to be willing to hop on the back of the steel horse [his motorcycle]! Sorry, that's a must!" *(InStyle)*

G "I like girls who make me laugh. Nice people get on with nice people. I just like people who are funny. Not too shy, but sometimes shy is cute." *(Twist)*

H "I'm an outdoorsy guy. I like to go camping and fishing. I'd like a girl who's into that stuff, too." *(Bop)*

Tyler Blackburn

Justin Bieber

Cody Simpson

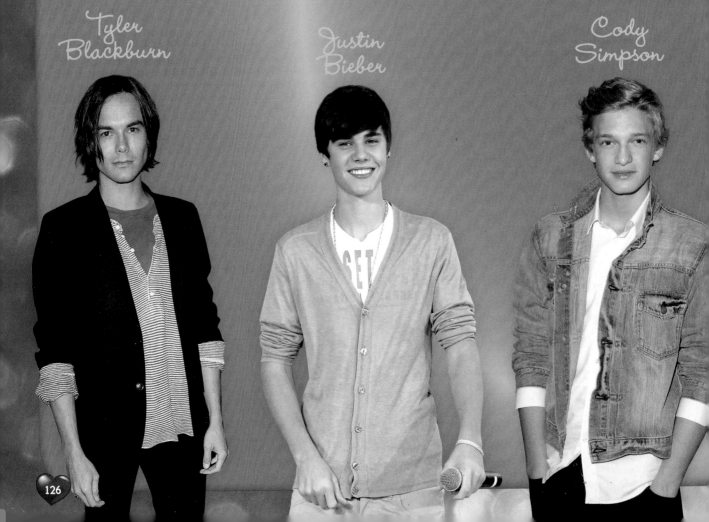

I

"I want to make sure I really get to know a girl when I like her. I flirt, but I take things slow. I don't want to rush anything." *(Tiger Beat)*

J

"It may seem cliché, but there's nothing wrong with bowling or movies or dinner or anything like that. I also like to do fun stuff too, like, we could go to the beach . . . I'd just think of different things that could just be fun for us and at the same time just be able to get to know each other better, just communicate." (hellobeautiful.com)

K

"I give out a lot of compliments! I notice things and call attention to what's great about her. I'm not afraid to say what's on my mind!" *(Bop)*

L

"I'm nice. I'd treat a girl well and I would buy her presents and take her to nice places. . . . If I really, really like them, then I'm loyal." *(Teen Now)*

Logan Henderson

Niall Horan

Diggy Simmons

Answers: A. Justin Bieber; B. James Maslow; C. Tyler Blackburn; D. Spencer Boldman; E. Taylor Lautner; F. Josh Hutcherson; G. Harry Styles; H. Nathan Kress; I. Cody Simpson; J. Diggy Simmons; K. Logan Henderson; L. Niall Horan.

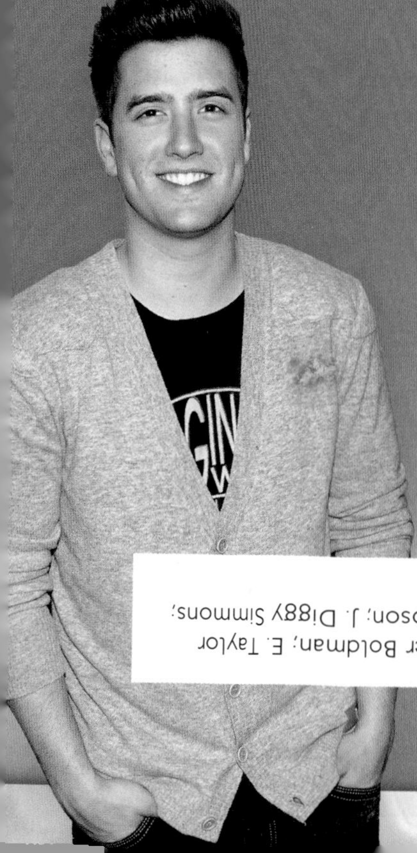

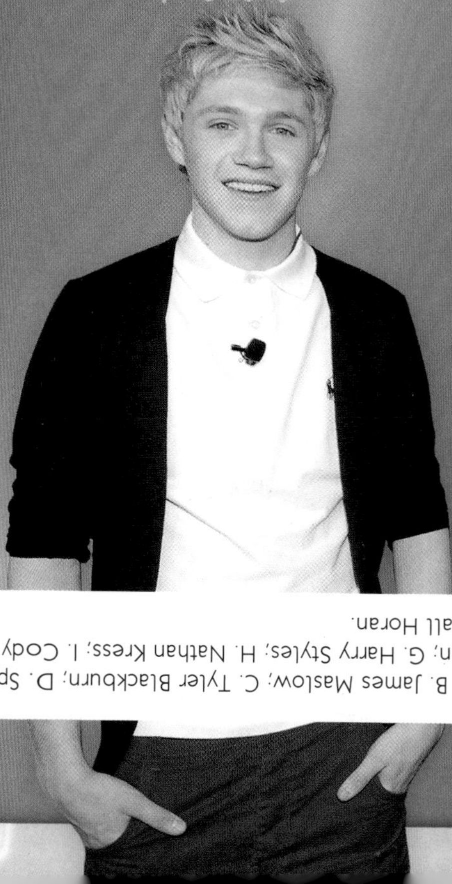

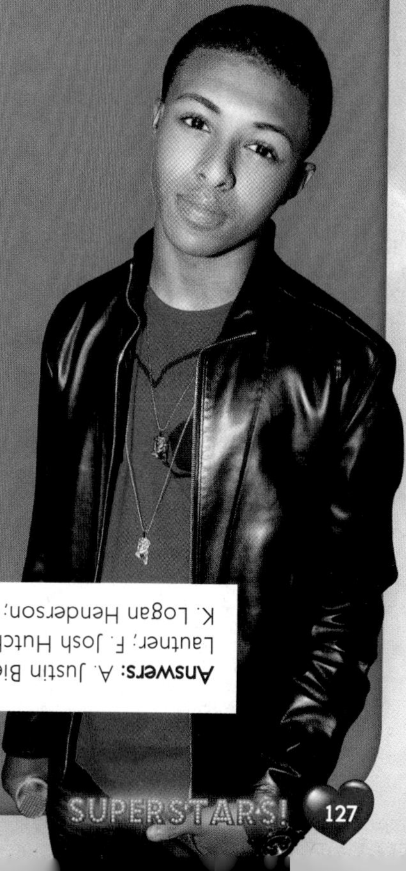

Front cover: Randy Holmes/Disney ABC Television Group/Getty Images (Bieber), Alberto E. Rodriguez/Getty Images (Big Time Rush), Sonia Recchia/WireImage/Getty Images (Hutcherson), Jon Furniss/WireImage/Getty Images (Mars), Newspix/Getty Images (One Direction). 2: Han Myung-Gu/WireImage/Getty Images (Kitsch), Victor Chavez/WireImage/Getty Images (Hutcherson), Angela Weiss/WireImage/Getty Images (Mars), David Becker/WireImage/Getty Images (Bieber). 3: AP Photo/Jonathan Short (Hemsworth), Raymond Boyd/Michael Ochs Archives/ Getty Images (Simmons), David Surowiecki/Getty Images (Kress), Christopher Polk/KCA2012/Getty Images (Lautner). 6: Jon Kopaloff/ FilmMagic/Getty Images. 7: PRNewsFoto/Nickelodeon, Katie Yu. 8: David Becker/WireImage/Getty Images. 9: Kevin Winter/Getty Images. 10: Randy Holmes/Disney ABC Television Group/Getty Images. 11: Kevork Djansezian/Getty Images (Bieber), © Splash News/Corbis (with Gomez), Kevin Winter/NBCUniversal/Getty Images (Swift). 12: AP Photo/Matt Sayles (Bieber), AP Photo/Arthur Mola (Jepsen). 14: Jason LaVeris/FilmMagic/Getty Images (Felton), AP Photo/Mark J. Terrill (Butler), Christopher Peterson/BuzzFoto/Getty Images (Garfield). 15: AP Photo/Joel Ryan (Pattinson), Noel Vasquez/Getty Images (Bieber), Michael Buckner/Getty Images (Hemsworth). 16: PRNewsFoto/ Nickelodeon, Katie Yu. 17: AP Photo/Carlo Allegri. 18: Jason Merritt/Getty Images. 19: Gabriel Olsen/FilmMagic/Getty Images. 20: Larry Busacca/Getty Images. 21: Jesse Grant/WireImage/Getty Images (top), Jim Spellman/WireImage/Getty Images (bottom). 22: Angela Weiss/ WireImage/Getty Images. 23: Kevin Winter/Getty Images. 24: X Factor/Getty Images. 25: Angela Weiss/WireImage/Getty Images. 26: Leon Neal/AFP/Getty Images. 27: Steve Granitz/WireImage/Getty Images. 28: Gregg DeGuire/FilmMagic/Getty Images (Butler), Pablo Blazquez Dominguez/WireImage/Getty Images (Efron), Sonia Recchia/WireImage/Getty Images (Hutcherson), Rabbani and Solimene/Getty Images (Hudgens). 29: Kevin Winter/Getty Images (Swift), Joey Foley/Getty Images (Lautner), Noel Vasquez/Getty Images (Collins), Jeffrey Mayer/ Getty Images (Gomez). 30: Jordan Strauss/WireImage/Getty Images. 31: NBC/NBCUniversal/Getty Images. 32: Gregg DeGuire/FilmMagic/ Getty Images. 33: Charley Gallay/WireImage/Getty Images (Big Help), Leon Bennett/WireImage/Getty Images (Thomas). 34: Valerie Macon/ Getty Images. 35: Jeff Vespa/WireImage/Getty Images. 36: Jason LaVeris/WireImage/Getty Images. 37: Bill McCay/WireImage/Getty Images. 38: Kevin Winter/Getty Images. 39: Jeff Vespa/WireImage/Getty Images. 40: Todd Williamson/WireImage/Getty Images. 41: Jeff Vespa/ WireImage/Getty Images. 42: Jordan Strauss/WireImage/Getty Images. 43: AP Photo/Matt Sayles. 44: Larry Marano/Getty Images. 45: Shirlaine Forrest/WireImage/Getty Images. 46: Larry Busacca/Getty Images. 47: Alberto E. Rodriguez/Getty Images. 48: Christopher Polk/ KCA2012/Getty Images. 49–50: Anita Bugge/WireImage/Getty Images (all). 51: Jason LaVeris/FilmMagic/Getty Images (Collins), Dominique Charriau/WireImage/Getty Images (Stewart), Kevork Djansezian/Getty Images (Lautner). 52–53: Christopher Polk/KCA2012/Getty Images (all). 54: Christopher Polk/WireImage/Getty Images. 55: Bob D'Amico/Disney ABC Television Group/Getty Images. 56–57: Paul Archuleta/ FilmMagic/Getty Images (all). 58: Mike Marsland/WireImage/Getty Images. 59: Donna Ward/Getty Images. 60: Sonia Recchia/WireImage/ Getty Images. 61: Eric Charbonneau/WireImage/Getty Images (with Lawrence), Graham Denholm/Getty Images (with Hudgens). 62: Victor Chavez/WireImage/Getty Images. 63: AP Photo/Arthur Mola. 64: Lester Cohen/WireImage/Getty Images. 65: John Shearer/Getty Images. 66: AP Photo/Jonathan Short. 67: AP Photo/Katy Winn. 68: John Kopaloff/FilmMagic/Getty Images. 69: AP Photo/Jennifer Graylock. 70: AP Photo/Katy Winn. 71: Steve Granitz/WireImage/Getty Images. 72: Jo Hale/Getty Images (Malik), Christopher Polk/KCA2012/Getty Images (Perry), Oleg Nikishin/Getty Images (Radcliffe), Jordan Strauss/WireImage/Getty Images (Bleu), Ethan Miller/Getty Images (Jolie). 73: Kevork Djansezian/Getty Images (Ludwig), Donato Sardella/WireImage/Getty Images (Alba), Larry Busacca/Getty Images (Banks), Hamish Blair/ Getty Images (Efron), JB Lacroix/WireImage/Getty Images (Cyrus), Jo Hale/Getty Images (Payne), Bennett Raglin/WireImage/Getty Images (Watson), Al Bello/Getty Images (Bieber). 74: Charles Eshelman/FilmMagic/Getty Images (Fox), Adam Pretty/Getty Images (Alba), Kevork Djansezian/Getty Images (Lautner), ChinaFotoPress/Getty Images (Chance), Ray Tamarra/Getty Images (Agron), Jason Merritt/Getty Images (Johansson), Jeffery Mayer/WireImage/Getty Images (McAdams), Jordan Strauss/WireImage/Getty Images (Lerman). 75: Todd Williamson/ Getty Images (Henrie), Dimitrios Kambouris/WireImage/Getty Images (Fox), Jason Merritt/Getty Images (Simpson, Gomez), Charley Gallay/ Getty Images (Beatty), Steve Granitz/WireImage/Getty Images (Grandel), Michael Buckner/Getty Images (Knight), Steve Granitz/WireImage/ Getty Images (Portman), Jon Kopaloff/FilmMagic/Getty Images (Johansson). 76: Jon Furniss/WireImage/Getty Images. 77: Dave J Hogan/ Getty Images. 78: Kevin Winter/Getty Images. 79: Ben Pruchnie/Getty Images (in a suit), AP Photo/Arthur Mola (talking). 80: Han Myung-Gu/ WireImage/Getty Images. 81: Dave J Hogan/Getty Images. 82: AP Photo/John Marshall JME. 83: Jon Kopaloff/FilmMagic/Getty Images. 84–85: Michael Buckner/WireImage/Getty Images. 86: Dave M. Benett/Getty Images. 87: Joseph Okpako/FilmMagic/Getty Images. 88: Jason LaVeris/FilmMagic/Getty Images (Posey, Wesley), Steve Granitz/WireImage/Getty Images (Simpson). 89: Paul Archuleta/FilmMagic/Getty Images (Musso), Michael Tran/Film Magic/Getty Images (Bleu), Charley Gallay/WireImage/Getty Images (Knight). 90: David Surowiecki/Getty Images. 91: Alberto E. Rodriguez/Getty Images. 92: Jeff Kardas/Getty Images. 93: Michael Tullberg/Getty Images. 94: Paul Morigi/Getty Images (with First Lady), Jordan Strauss/WireImage/Getty Images (wave). 95: Paul Morigi/Getty Images. 96: Rebecca Sapp/WireImage/Getty Images. 97: Alli Harvey/Getty Images. 98: Jordan Strauss/WireImage/Getty Images. 99: Alli Harvey/Getty Images. 100: Gilbert Carrasquillo/ WireImage. 101: Toby Canham/Getty Images. 102: Michael Buckner/Getty Images (headshot), Angela Weiss/Getty Images (green sweater). 103: AP Photo/Chris Pizzello (all). 104: Jason LaVeris/FilmMagic/Getty Images (suit), Steve Granitz/WireImage/Getty Images (sunglasses). 105: Jordan Strauss/WireImage/Getty Images (headshot), Jason LaVeris/FilmMagic/Getty Images (hands in pockets). 106: Johnny Nunez/ WireImage/Getty Images. 107: Taylor Hill/FilmMagic/Getty Images. 108: Johnny Nunez/WireImage/Getty Images. 109–110: Raymond Boyd/ Michael Ochs Archives/Getty Images (all). 111: Bennett Raglin/Getty Images. 112: Jon Furniss/WireImage/Getty Images (Hemsworth), Jeffery Mayer/WireImage/Getty Images (Monteith). 113: Jesse Grant/WireImage/Getty Images. 114: David Livingston/Getty Images (Dano), Frazer Harrison/Getty Images (Knight). 115: Hamish Blair/Getty Images (Efron), Jason LaVeris/FilmMagic/Getty Images (Henrie), David Becker/WireImage/Getty Images (Till). 117: Larry Marano/FilmMagic/Getty Images (Jonas), John Grieshop/Getty Images (Hutcherson), Mike Coppola/Getty Images (Kress). 118: Jason Merritt/Getty Images. 119: David Becker/Getty Images (Unger), Beck Starr/FilmMagic/Getty Images (Stewart). 120: Imeh Akpanudosen/Getty Images (Wesley), BuzzFoto/Getty Images (Butler). 121: Charley Gallay/KCA2012/Getty Images (with RDJ), Albert L. Ortega/Getty Images (Dekker). 122: David Livingston/Getty Images (Miller), Robyn Beck/AFP/Getty Images (Dolley). 123: Gustavo Caballero/Getty Images (Ludwig), Frazer Harrison/Getty Images (Knight). 124: Victor Chavez/WireImage/Getty Images (Hutcherson), Jo Hale/Getty Images (Styles), Jeff Vespa/WireImage/Getty Images (Boldman). 125: Mike Coppola/Getty Images (Lautner), Larry Busacca/Getty Images (Maslow), David Surowiecki/Getty Images (Kress). 126: Jason LaVeris/WireImage/Getty Images (Blackburn), AP Photo/Matt Sayles (Bieber), Rebecca Sapp/ WireImage/Getty Images (Simpson). 127: AP Photo/Peter Kramer (Big Time Rush), Larry Busacca/Getty Images (Horan), Johnny Nunez/ WireImage/Getty Images (Simmons). Back cover: Bennett Raglin/Getty Images (Simmons), Alli Harvey/Getty Images (Simpson), David Livingston/Getty Images (Kitsch), Fotonoticias/WireImage/Getty Images (Efron), Jason Merritt/Getty Images (Big Time Rush).